The PhD Experience

D0910832

www.palgravestudyskills.com – the leading study skills website

Palgrave Student to Student
How to Get a First *Michael Tefula*
The PhD Experience *Evelyn Barron*
Student Brain Food *Lauren Lucien*
Student Procrastination *Michael Tefula*
Studying as a Parent *Helen Owton*
University Life *Lauren Lucien*

You may also be interested in the following by Palgrave:
Authoring a PhD *Patrick Dunleavy*
Completing Your PhD *Kate Williams et al.*
The Foundations of Research (2nd edn) *Jonathan Grix*
Getting to Grips with Doctoral Research *Margaret Walshaw*
Getting Published *Gina Wisker*
The Good Supervisor (2nd edn) *Gina Wisker*
The PhD Viva *Peter Smith*
Planning Your PhD *Kate Williams et al.*
The Postgraduate Research Handbook (2nd edn) *Gina Wisker*

For a complete listing of all titles in our Study Skills range please visit
www.palgrave.com/studyskills

The PhD Experience

An Insider's Guide

Evelyn Barron

Schaumburg Township District Library
130 South Roselle Road
Schaumburg, Illinois 60193

© Evelyn Barron 2014

All rights reserved. No reproduction, copy or transmission of this publication may be made without written permission.

No portion of this publication may be reproduced, copied or transmitted save with written permission or in accordance with the provisions of the Copyright, Designs and Patents Act 1988, or under the terms of any licence permitting limited copying issued by the Copyright Licensing Agency, Saffron House, 6–10 Kirby Street, London EC1N 8TS.

Any person who does any unauthorized act in relation to this publication may be liable to criminal prosecution and civil claims for damages.

The author has asserted her right to be identified as the author of this work in accordance with the Copyright, Designs and Patents Act 1988.

First published 2014 by
PALGRAVE
Palgrave Macmillan in the UK is an imprint of Macmillan Publishers Limited, registered in England, company number 785998, of 4 Crinan Street, London N1 9XW

Palgrave Macmillan in the US is a division of St Martin's Press LLC, 175 Fifth Avenue, New York, NY 10010.

Palgrave is a global imprint of the above companies and is represented throughout the world.

Palgrave® and Macmillan® are registered trademarks in the United States, the United Kingdom, Europe and other countries.

ISBN: 978-1-137-38384-6

This book is printed on paper suitable for recycling and made from fully managed and sustained forest sources. Logging, pulping and manufacturing processes are expected to conform to the environmental regulations of the country of origin.

A catalogue record for this book is available from the British Library.

A catalog record for this book is available from the Library of Congress.

Printed in China

Contents

Acknowledgements

Thanks to Kathleen, David and Ben for their support while writing this book and in general.

Thanks also to Adi, Alistair, Ben, Claire, David, Fiona, Fiza, Helen (both of you), Josephine, Lisa (both of you), Nadezhda, Ravi, Rebecca, Sarah, Sebastian, Stephanie and all those who have chosen to remain anonymous for sharing your experiences with me, as well as everyone at Palgrave for their support throughout this process.

Introduction

Purpose of the book

The main purpose of this book is to illustrate what the experience of undertaking a PhD in the UK system can be like; however, many aspects will be applicable to PhD students worldwide. I hope that the information contained within will encourage prospective PhD students to think carefully about what being a PhD student will mean apart from the academic work – I wish there had been someone to tell me these things and help me be more prepared! I also hope that this book will be useful to current PhD students at various stages of completion who may find themselves in situations where they can benefit from the previous experience of those people who I have quoted here. Third, any PhD student, prospective or current, would benefit from having their family, friends, or anyone in their support network read this book as well. PhDs can be a very challenging time for any student, and support and understanding will be needed along the way. Finally, I hope this book will give those outside the academic process an idea about what PhD students do and the challenges we face, and an understanding of how important our support network can be.

What this book does

This book will give you a clear, concise and honest picture about the reality of being a PhD student, both inside and outside of academic life, from the initial decision to undertake a PhD, through the various stages along the way, to the decisions about what comes next. What this book will not do is go into any depth about methods for completing your work. If you want to know more about study design, reviewing the literature, conducting statistical analysis or writing up a PhD thesis, there are many other good books available out there which will be specific to your subject and guide you through the process step by step.

There are, of course, other guides available to help you through the process of being a PhD student; however, the benefit of this book is the focus on experience. Many books are written by seasoned academics who are many years removed from their student days. Although they have a wealth of valuable experience to share, they tend to focus on the point of view of the academic process. Before starting my PhD, I did not know any other PhD students; I wish I had been able to talk to those who were going through it too and shared my perspective, who could have told me about the day-to-day reality of doing a PhD.

This book is based on the real-life experiences, both good and bad, of current and recent PhD students. As a PhD student myself, I have access to a variety of individuals who are currently undertaking their PhDs or who have recently completed one. This has allowed me to get opinions on various topics from people with a wide range of different backgrounds, working at different stages of the process in different fields and in different institutions. These people have generously shared their stories so that you can benefit from their experiences, and I have included some of my own experiences too. PhD study comes with highs and lows, good times and bad times. Some of the quotes given could be perceived as sensitive or negative; therefore, in order to allow people to be completely honest in their expression, only first names and ages are given so that the students cannot be easily identified by their supervisors and to protect the anonymity of their institutions. Some people have chosen to use a pseudonym, indicated by an asterisk, but regardless of the name on the quote, the experience behind it is real.

How to use this book

Please do not feel that you have to read this book from beginning to end in one go. The chapters are broken up in such a way that you can dip in and out of what is relevant to you at particular times during your studies.

Chapter 1 examines the reasons for wanting to do a PhD and discusses the attributes which can help to make you a successful PhD student.

Chapter 2 looks at the decisions you need to make in order to be a PhD student, including the choices to be made about universities, supervisors and your project, as well as practical arrangements like finding a place to live, finances and how to prepare for an interview.

Chapter 3 considers the timing of becoming a PhD student and the pros and cons of starting a PhD at different stages of your career.

Chapter 4 looks at the different formats a PhD can take and the different routes of PhD study available. The various ways of funding PhDs are also discussed here.

Chapter 5 separates out the beginning, middle and concluding stages of a PhD project and discusses issues specific to each stage, such as the research proposal, writing up and looking for jobs. Tips are given from students' past experiences of dealing with these issues. This chapter also considers the viva and what happens if not everything goes according to plan.

Chapter 6 talks about the realities of doing a PhD project, such as maintaining interest and motivation, knowing how much of your time you should expect to devote to your work, having strategies to manage your time and, ultimately, whether or not being a PhD student is enjoyable. Information about what you can expect from supervisors is also given here as well as what your supervisors will expect from you and what to do if you encounter problems.

Chapter 7 looks at sources of support such as your institution and colleagues as well as family and friends. Working conditions are discussed: the daily routine, fieldwork, office politics, pressures and holidays.

Chapter 8 focuses on additional demands on your time which you may not have thought of as part of your PhD, such as producing publications and attending conferences, training courses and public engagement activities.

Chapter 9 focuses on life outside of your PhD, including personal finances, leisure time, the effect of PhD study on relationships, and social support. This chapter also includes a look at what happens next, post-PhD.

Finally, a list of useful websites is provided to point you in the right direction for additional details and further information.

The journey

The journey towards achieving your PhD can be testing and rewarding and will probably be both at one time or another, but hopefully reading about the lessons learnt by other PhD students will help you feel more prepared to take it all on. Your confidence and skills will improve year on year, and the feeling of most students is, 'If I can do it, anyone can!'

Why Do a PhD?

Reasons for doing a PhD

The fact that you are reading this book suggests that you already have some reasons for wanting to do a PhD. But are you sure? Are your reasons good ones or will you look back in a year's time and wish you had chosen differently?

I asked all of the people who gave me a quote for this book why they had decided to do a PhD and the answers I got back could be divided into two main themes: employment prospects and enjoyment of the work. Employment-related reasons for doing a PhD included the following:

- not many graduate jobs available so a PhD is something else to do in the meantime;
- wanting to improve future job prospects;
- avoiding entering the job market in the current economic climate;
- wanting to go into academia;
- wanting a career in research;
- wanting to become an independent researcher;
- wanting to gain additional skills in their chosen field;
- their chosen career path requires it – they need a PhD to do a particular job or to get a promotion.

Reasons related to enjoyment included:

- they enjoyed lectures and reading about the field, so wanted to study it further;
- they had a good time doing a Master's degree and wanted to carry on;

- they are interested in the subject;
- they are interested in research;
- they enjoyed the research component of their undergraduate dissertation and wanted to carry on.

Other reasons given for doing a PhD included developing and improving research skills, gaining new knowledge, becoming an expert in a chosen field, the availability of scholarships, because friends were also doing PhDs and, finally, not being sure what else to do.

One of the most interesting things about this exercise was that everyone came back to me with at least two answers; not a single person only had one reason for doing a PhD. Some of the reasons people gave may seem better than others. For example, doing a PhD because your friends are doing one might not be the best motivation, nor enough to sustain you through the entire project, whereas 'to become an expert in the field' seems like a pretty sound answer, on paper at least. In reality, almost everyone mentioned a practical issue such as needing expertise on a topic or the research skills from a PhD to embark upon their chosen career or get a particular job, or needing a scholarship to be available to allow them to be able to do a PhD.

Career-wise, having a PhD can be a necessary requirement of a job or career. Some industry jobs require people to have the research skills you develop during a PhD, while in other careers, such as academia, you will not be able to progress very far up the ladder without one. In contrast, wanting a PhD for the sake of being called 'Dr' is probably not a good reason. Another reason for doing a PhD, and indeed a trait that will help you get through one, is a love of learning. If you do not still enjoy learning, a PhD will be an uphill struggle.

Doing a PhD gives you a taste of what life is like as a researcher and as an academic, allowing you to either rule out or consider these careers more seriously. You should have opportunities to get involved with teaching, so you can also consider this as an option. Through attending conferences and training courses and so on, you will be able to build up a network of contacts working in your area of interest. By using professional networking sites you can keep an eye on the various skills your peers are training in and see the publications they are bringing out, and so keep an eye on the competition. Contacts will also be useful when it comes to looking for jobs after the PhD and these contacts are likely to be from sectors outside of the university setting. The time you spend doing your PhD project and the experiences you get along the way will help to inform your future career choices.

Reasons for undertaking a PhD are personal and different for everyone, but whatever your reasons are, be sure before you start that they are good enough to keep you going through the whole project.

Advantages and disadvantages of a PhD

There are both advantages and disadvantages to undertaking a PhD and the chances are you will come across many of each during your time as a PhD student. The experience of being a PhD student varies considerably from individual to individual but it is important to consider up front what you might be facing. One significant advantage of doing a PhD, no matter what you choose to do next, is the skill set you will acquire and improve upon along the way. Through writing up your thesis and, hopefully, getting some work published as you go, your writing and analytical skills should improve considerably. Presentations are a large part of being a PhD student and you will learn to become more polished, flexible and confident in your abilities to present to various audiences, whether to your own research group or at an international conference full of senior experts. Your self-discipline will also improve – for most people this is a necessity or they would not finish! While you are a PhD student you will be doing original research, on a topic you enjoy, and will continually be learning new things. You will get to work with experts in your field as well as building up a professional network of contacts from both inside and outside of academia who may well be able to point you towards jobs and serve as referees for job applications later on. To a large extent, you will be working independently: it will be up to you what shape your day's work will take and you will have the freedom to manage your own time, which can give you some flexibility in your schedule. Day to day, you will be working with other very intelligent people and often interesting characters. You may well get the opportunity to travel – for example, to conferences – and you may have the opportunity to try some teaching. This extended period of being a student can also act as a buffer to give you time to make important decisions about your future career and job prospects; and the skills you have learnt during this time will give you more career choices and may help you achieve a higher salary and position than would otherwise have been available. Never forget that a PhD is very hard work, so you can take pride in the fact that you are doing something that the majority of people will never do by making an original contribution to the field, and take satisfaction in seeing a finished project which you have worked hard on. You are turning yourself into an expert.

So, with all of those good points, what possible disadvantages could there be to doing a PhD? There are several things to be aware of. First of all, there is the course itself. If you go into a PhD expecting it to be a slightly harder version of an undergraduate or Master's degree, you will be in for an unpleasant surprise. At PhD level, you are expected to generate new ideas and this can place significant pressure on you, as can deadlines for various stages of your project and the focus on producing results. Aside from pressure, there is also the additional emotional impact. Working independently can be a positive experience, but after a while it can lead to a feeling of isolation. Similarly, the highs and lows of a PhD project can be an emotionally draining experience, and this can be compounded by the sacrifice of your family and social life you will very likely have to make due to the time your PhD project takes up, especially towards the end of the process. Time commitment is another disadvantage of PhDs, whether the long hours expended on your work means a reduced social life, or the long block of time you spend being a PhD student means you enter the workforce at a greater age while your peers have been getting promoted through the ranks. By doing a PhD you are making a trade-off of your time, the salary you could have been earning if you were working instead of doing the PhD and any fees you are paying against potentially higher earnings in the future. Remember also that there are very few financial rewards to be gained during a PhD.

You may be able to earn a little money from teaching, but this will take time away from your project; and it is important to remember that you do not earn anything from any publications you produce, such as journal articles. Also, take into account that having a PhD is not a guarantee of earning more in the long run; you must be sure you will not be making yourself overqualified for a particular job you might want in the future.

What makes a good PhD student?

There are certain attributes which it is an advantage to possess and which are more likely to help you become a successful PhD student. This is not a prescriptive or an exhaustive list, however, as everyone is different and will have their own strengths and weaknesses.

Making a contribution to the field

The primary aim of your PhD work is to make an original contribution to the field you are working in either by pushing the boundaries of your field or solving a particular problem within it. The easy part, usually done by doing a lot of reading up on the area, is identifying where the boundaries currently are or what the problems are which need to be solved for your field to advance ... but the hard part is resolving these problems. If it was not difficult, it would have been done already. The harder part still is convincing other experts in the area, as well as your examiners, that you have made a meaningful contribution. This also links to your communication skills, whether in written or verbal format. To be a successful PhD student you will need to hone your ability to persuade others. You will need to be able to persuade your supervisors that your ideas have been well thought through and your lines of enquiry are worth pursuing. You will need to be able to persuade your assessors and eventually your examiners that you have made a valid contribution to the field, and you will need to persuade other researchers that you have done the same thing – for instance, at conferences. As well as being persuasive, you will also need to be able to communicate the key messages from your research very clearly at the level appropriate for your audience (i.e., expert versus non-expert). In general, people will pay more attention to your work if you minimise the effort they need to expend in understanding the important points. There is a high probability that during the course of your PhD some of your attempts to answer the questions you set out to answer will not work. This is the point when you need to persevere.

What can help you to be successful?

Throughout your studies it will help you if you maintain a sense of realism about what you can achieve within the time and budget allowed. You will also need to be realistic about how much impact your project will make: it is much more likely that you will make an important but modest contribution to your field rather than redefine the area. Also, remember that a PhD is the academic version of an apprenticeship: you will be expected to have a certain level of skill at the start but you do not need to be perfect straight away. Your finished thesis will also not be perfect, but this is all right as long as you are able to demonstrate that you are aware of what the strengths and limitations of your work are, and to show that you have learnt from your mistakes and would know what you could do to improve your project if you were to do it again.

Self-management

Knowing how to manage your time is a key factor in being a successful PhD student. Setting goals and knowing what the priorities are in your work is important, but be realistic about how much time each goal will take. Similarly, being able to evaluate your progress towards these goals is a critical skill which you will need in order to stay on target. As you move forward with your research, new studies emerging in the field and the data you obtain can spark ideas for new directions in which to take your project. You will need to evaluate whether exploring these new directions is a good use of your time or simply a tangent you could be distracted by, and it can be helpful to keep a written record of how and why you make these decisions. Keeping good records from the very beginning of your project will help you answer your supervisors' questions and aid you with the writing up. It is very easy to think that it is not worth noting down something which seems minor because you are convinced you will remember it, but chances are you will quickly forget the finer details – and who knows how important those details will become later on!

PhD students are expected to, and must, work hard – but there is a big difference between working hard and working effectively. As noted earlier, it is important to enjoy the work that you are doing, and if you have enthusiasm for your work, working hard on it should not be a problem. At this level of study you are expected to manage your own learning and become increasingly independent. You must take responsibility for your own work, for how you organise your time and your project – it is your project and no one will do it for you. There may be times when you need to rein in this same enthusiasm in order to be sure not to overcommit yourself. During your studies you may be exposed to various opportunities to develop your skills, gain some experience or perhaps earn some money, but always consider how much time these things will take away from your project, which is the reason you are there in the first place.

Communication

Another essential for all PhD students is good communication skills, whether in written or verbal form. A key to success is the ability to communicate clearly and effectively with your supervisors. It will help you if you can quickly learn your supervisors' working style. You must also be able to manage your supervisors' expectations and how to negotiate your progress – for example, when it is time to move on to the next part of your project. Take responsibility for making sure that regular supervision meetings are arranged.

A measure of how successful a PhD student has been is how many papers they have published and the quality of the journals they have published in, but rejection rates in some journals are high, so persevere! If you are considering a career in academia, be aware that having a PhD in itself is not enough anymore, so get working on those publications!

Writing is another facet to your success as a PhD student. You may already feel confident in your writing abilities. You may even already have some published work; however, there is always room for improvement. Learn to write as you go. By doing this you avoid the risk of forgetting the central meaning of whatever you have recently been reading or thinking about. Get into the habit of writing detailed notes to record your ideas, which will later help form your thesis and/or journal articles. It will also help you to focus and keep your project on track as well as helping you to reflect on what you have done so far so that you can see how you can improve your project. The more you write, the more your writing will improve. This way, by the time you get to writing up the final version of your thesis your writing style will have come on by leaps and bounds, however good it was when you started out. Alongside writing up often comes procrastination. Be aware of this and find out quickly what helps you to avoid it. This is different for everyone but might include breaks, bribery, set working times, positive or negative reinforcement and the removal of distractions, for example closing your email until you have accomplished a particular task.

The procrastination problem

Procrastination can be a problem in many areas of life, but it can be especially detrimental to your PhD studies. This is particularly true in the first year of your PhD, when the time left until you must submit seems to be stretching way into the distance. Many books, blogs, newspaper articles and web pages have been written about the nature of procrastination and strategies to overcome it. When you have a piece of work to start, especially if it is something arduous or not particularly exciting, it is amazing how many other little tasks you can find to do first. Often these tasks are quite necessary, so spending your time on those before starting your intended piece of work can seem legitimate; however, it is amazing how much progress with your actual work you can lose out on because of this avoidance. It is important to break the procrastination habit as early as possible, otherwise it is likely to increase the levels of stress and pressure you feel during your studies and could potentially stay with you for the rest of your career.

I used to be one of those people who thought they worked better under a bit of time pressure, and up to a certain point this strategy worked well for me. Things always got done to a good enough standard, so I had plenty of time for procrastination. Before really settling down to do some work, there were emails to check or news headlines to have a quick look at. But then, since I was on the Internet anyway, there were always a few more websites I had been meaning to have a look at. Oh, and while I was on, I might as well order some grocery shopping, look up cinema times for the weekend, maybe see if there are any bargains to be had … And so it goes on. The trouble with a PhD project is that it does not leave time for procrastination. This can be deceptive at the start when you still have your whole project stretched ahead of you, but time really does fly. Suddenly the time pressure is constant, so the procrastination has to go. Find ways to motivate yourself. For me, making 'to do' lists and breaking tasks down into smaller pieces of work with deadlines helped because being able to tick things off as I went along gave me a sense of achievement. And feeling that you have achieved something feels much better than being under pressure!

Another quality of successful PhD students is that they know when they need to ask for help, whether from supervisors, experts in a particular techniques, specialists in your methodology or your peers. Asking for help is not an admission of failure and can often help avoid exactly that. Many PhD students lack confidence in themselves or their abilities at some point during their studies, but you need to believe that you can keep going and get your PhD even when it feels impossible. Some PhD students report feeling like a fraud because they do not think they are clever enough to be doing a PhD. You do not need to be a genius – and if you were not clever enough to do a PhD you would not have made it far enough to be thinking about doing one. One strategy to keep your confidence up is to avoid comparing yourself to everyone else. Remind yourself that the grass always looks greener on the other side, and however brilliantly someone appears to be doing on the surface, you do not know that they are not feeling exactly the same as you. Everyone has good and bad patches throughout their studies. Remember – you are not in competition with anyone.

Finally, being a good PhD student does not just mean working hard and having high productivity. Keep some perspective and make sure you take some time out for yourself so that you do not burn out.

2

Decisions to Be Made

Once you have decided that you want to do a PhD, you have more decisions to make. Which university should you study at? What are priorities in terms of location, facilities or reputation of staff? Who will supervise your project? What will the focus of your project be? How will you pay the fees? Do you need funding? Where will you live?

University

Just as universities may interview prospective PhD students to make sure they are taking on the right candidates, it is important to make sure you are choosing the best university for your needs. It may be that you are limited to a particular geographical area for financial reasons or family commitments, but if you have the freedom to move to the 'best' university then there are a few points you can consider. These include the research quality ranking of the university and department you are interested in, the facilities available to you, the research interests and reputation of staff and what else is going on in your area of study.

Most, if not all, universities will have a page on their website called 'Why study at ...?' or 'Why choose us?' or something similar. These pages tend to start by talking about the university's reputation, the quality of research and teaching, the quality of the facilities and the highlights of the city where the university is based. The quality of the university could be an important factor in your decision and there are some measures of quality out there to help you compare universities. The Russell Group (**www.russellgroup.ac.uk**) is a collection of 24 British universities which are widely considered some of the most prestigious in the country,

> ☺ **Inside view**
>
> The university I completed my LLB [qualifying law degree] at were advertising funding so I applied for that. I did not look at any other universities or courses and, looking back, it would have been good to compare what was available in different places, as the department was not ideal for my research area (although this was overcome by having joint supervision with a different department). My original proposal was on one adult social care topic but, over my Master's and PhD, the topic and focus has completely changed.
>
> *Sarah, 28*

receiving a large proportion of research grants and awarding around half of PhDs in the UK. Another useful indicator of quality of research in UK institutions is the Research Excellence Framework (**www.ref.ac.uk**). From 2014 the REF will replace the RAE (Research Assessment Exercise) and grade universities on a star system, from 'unclassified' at the bottom end of the scale to four stars for being world leading in terms of research.

It is a good idea to have a look at the background and research interests of the other staff in the department, as you are likely to end up working either directly with them or alongside them and learning from them. What are their areas of expertise? How closely does their work tie in with what you are doing? How good is their publication record? If at all possible, try and talk to the people in the research group you will be joining about the department to get a sense of what it might be like to work there.

Another thing to consider is the facilities provided by the university. What is important here will vary from person to person and might not even be something you are considering in your search for a university, but it is nonetheless important. Start by working out what kinds of facilities are important to you. For example, if you have your own computer, the university's IT facilities might not feature prominently on your list. Are the libraries' opening hours important to you? Think about any specialist technical facilities or software that are necessary for your research. How easy will it be to gain access to these? What about study support such as writing development or help with statistics? You may also want to consider the day-to-day working environment. Will you get your own desk or are you expected to 'hot desk' or find your own space to work from? What kind of administrative support will you be provided with? Development opportunities might be another factor in your decision. What development opportunities or training courses does the university have on offer and do they have a cost attached? If so, would it be you or your department who pays? Do you want opportunities to get teaching experience? What training would be provided for this? Would you be able to get any formal teaching qualifications if this is something you are interested in? There are also non-academic university-based facilities and events you could consider. Does the university have good student support facilities, such as pastoral and financial advice, a careers service or access to religious services? If fitness is important to you, perhaps a university gym would be a plus. If you are interested in culture, are there any dramatic or musical performances, public lectures, museums or art galleries attached to the university? Does the Students' Union have special events for postgraduates? Are there any societies you are interested in?

Choosing the right university for your PhD studies might mean a move to a different city, so it is important that you are happy with what the city in question has to offer. University websites often have pages detailing why the city they are in is a good place to live, but these are often aimed at undergraduates and you might be looking for more. You could also look up rankings of student experience, but these often pertain to an undergraduate experience and it is likely your priorities will have changed a bit by the time you become a postgraduate. Think about what you want out of the city. Do you want culture, shopping, sport or nightlife, or a mixture of all of these? Living costs can also influence the choice you have over the area you live in. What kind of accommodation can you get for your budget and is this suitable for your particular needs? What is the public transport or car parking like? How much will it cost in both and money and time to make trips home? These are all easy enough questions to answer with a little bit of research and perhaps a short visit before you make your final decision, but there is no substitute for talking to someone who has lived in the area for a while.

Supervisors

This is arguably the most important choice you will be faced with since your supervisors will play a large role in determining whether your PhD experience is a positive one. Whether you are looking for a supervisor to oversee a project you are applying for funding for, or looking into a named supervisor on an advertised project, it is advisable to make sure as far as possible that they are a good fit for both you and your work. When looking for a potential supervisor, or looking into a potential supervisor if you are going for an advertised project, the most obvious place to start is their profile page on the university website. These pages often give a short description of the person's contact details, qualifications, research interests, positions of responsibility (for example, roles within the department, memberships of governing bodies and advisory panels), teaching responsibilities, areas of supervision and recent publication record. Reading their most recent journal articles can give you valuable insight into the nature of their academic work and their current research interests. Does their work excite you? Positions of responsibility can indicate whether or not the person is respected within their field and will reflect their degree of expertise and experience.

Of course, web pages and journal articles can only tell you about the professional life of your potential supervisor and very little about their personality or even what they will be like to work with. As a student, you want to know that your supervisor has enough available time to give you the guidance that you require. There may be a trade-off between the level of experience your supervisor has and the time they have available for you, depending on where they are at in their career. A seasoned professor with a few teaching commitments, several postgraduate students, leading roles in a portfolio of research groups and appointments to myriad boards and committees will have a wealth of experience to share but may be quite time poor. On the other hand, a relatively young academic who is still very 'hands on' with research may be able to offer you more time and practical help on a day-to-day basis but will not have the decades of experience of the ins and outs of research and supervising students that a more senior supervisor is likely to have. These two are at opposite ends of a spectrum, and of course there are many people in between, but there are advantages and disadvantages to each and you need to think about who you would gain the most from. Of course, if you have more than one supervisor perhaps all of these bases will be covered. You also want to know whether you will be able to have a good working relationship with this person; after all, you will be spending three or more years of your life working alongside them. Unfortunately, knowing what your relationship with your supervisors will be like will only come from experience. However, it might influence your decision if you can talk to the supervisor's current or recent past students to see if they had a positive experience and find out a bit about your potential supervisor's working style and communication style. Does this person sound like someone you could work with? Likewise, for other staff in the department, look at their publication record and what projects they are involved in, both currently and in the past. Would it be possible to meet with anyone in the department? It is important that you can work well with these people too. Do they seem happy with the department, facilities and working hours? How many papers do they publish? Have they been given the opportunity to be first author on any papers?

Supervisors tend to be very busy people and therefore you might not have much of an opportunity to talk to them before applying for your PhD, with even less opportunity for students applying for an advertised project rather than working on a proposal in conjunction with the supervisor. In the case of applying for an advertised studentship, it is advisable to make contact with your supervisor early in the application process to register your interest in the studentship. If you are going to try and make contact with a potential supervisor, what kind of contact will this be? Are you going to ask for a face-to-face meeting or a teleconference, or will email suffice? Most supervisors can be contacted directly but in some instances they may have a secretary or personal assistant who may be your initial contact. In reality, email is the most likely, especially for a first contact, which can then be followed up with a teleconference or face-to-face meeting if required.

In any form of contact, you need to leave your potential supervisor with a good impression of you. If you are going to email them, use a formal tone and keep it short; remember that they are most likely time poor. Provide some background on yourself and include a CV as an attached file in case they want any more information. Be specific about why you have got in touch, show you know something about their work and do not be afraid to ask questions. However, make sure you do not simply ask questions which could easily be answered by rereading the studentship description or the university website, as this will not reflect well on your abilities as a potential PhD student. You could ask any of the questions included in the 'Preparing for an interview' section, but other information you might also be interested in may include: How many other students have they supervised? Have all of these students completed on time and what have they gone on to do? How often can you expect to have contact with your supervisor? Who would they recommend as a second supervisor (or, who is in place as a second supervisor if applying for an advertised project?)? Do they plan to be available for the entirety of your time as a student, or are they planning a sabbatical, retirement or a move to a different institution? What do they expect the main outcomes of your PhD project to be?

Project

No matter what type of PhD you want to do, and no matter how you plan to fund it, selecting the right PhD project for you is essential. You are going to spend a small but significant proportion of your life working on this topic, so make sure it is something you will enjoy, maintain interest in for the duration and that meets your reasons for wanting to do a PhD in the first place.

⬭⬭⬭ **Inside view**

Before applying to PhDs I did a lot of looking around, trying to find something that really interested me – something a little unusual and different. I ended up finding a project that sounded great, and it was combining my interests in imaging and genetics. The real kicker was that it was going to be using a microscope that, at the time, was only set up in three different labs in Europe, and the supervisor was going to support me while I developed my programming skills.

Jack, 26

There is more than one route to finding a PhD project, but the Internet is a good place to start. FindAPhD.com is a searchable database of available PhDs in the UK and abroad. You can search by discipline, subject, keywords, location, institution, PhD programme type (for example, four-year programme, international, doctoral training centre) and funding. Jobs.ac.uk works along similar lines. If you already have a shortlist of institutions you wish to work at, have a look at the postgraduate sections of their websites. These should provide you with details of any advertised projects, and details of departments that are currently welcoming applications (where the project may be more negotiable). They will also give details of fees, entrance requirements, guidance on how to apply and details of potential funding. Discipline-specific magazines also sometimes have PhD opportunities tucked away among the job advertisements, so it is worth keeping an eye on these too. Word of mouth can also be a great way to find out about PhD projects. If you are currently a student or are working in academia, or know someone who is, it could be worth asking around to find out if any academics might be looking to take on a PhD student, or if someone has just been awarded a grant and could afford to take on a PhD student.

Typically, there are two ways of getting a PhD project: by applying for an advertised project, or by applying for funding for your own project idea. Applying for an advertised project has the advantage of being fairly straightforward, as you identify the project you feel you have the relevant skills to do well at and enough enthusiasm for the topic to spend a long time working on it and follow the application process set out by the institution where you would be based. This is often accompanied by guidelines on how to complete the application process and details about what points you should cover in your personal statement and application form and so on. However, advertised projects often come with just a very short description of what the project will be about and what the funders want you to achieve. You will still have to come up with your own ideas on how to achieve the aims of the project and there may be some scope for you to add your own ideas on how to conduct the research.

On the other hand, you could apply to do a project of your own design. This is a little less straightforward because it involves identifying a supervisor who is willing to take you on, coming up with a research proposal and applying for funding for the project, or putting your own funding in place if you intend to self-fund (applying for funding will be discussed in more detail later in this chapter). Before contacting a potential supervisor you should have an argument prepared for why this person should give you their time and why your proposed work is important. However, this option does give you a little more freedom to decide on the direction and ultimate goals of your research, although you will need to be prepared to be flexible and negotiate changes to the direction and methodology of the project with your supervisor.

Both types of project will involve a research proposal at some point. When applying for funding for a project you will have to submit a research proposal, and even when you go for an advertised project you will still need to submit a formal document of your proposed work. There is no set way of writing a research proposal and there are lots of books available to give you subject-specific guidance. In general, your research proposal should contain your hypotheses, aims, objectives and research questions, which should be specific enough to be answerable during the time frame of your studentship. You should also demonstrate the gap in the current literature which you are addressing and how you aim to fill it, why it is important to fill this gap, how your planned research fits in with the key literature and any new work which is coming out, in what way your work is original and what the implications are for the general public. You will also need to give details of the methods you plan to use to answer your research questions, a time scale for the project (a diagram such as a Gantt chart can often be helpful here) and a discussion of the resources you intend to use. The development of the research proposal does not need to be a solitary activity. This stage is a great time to seek advice from specialists in the area to make sure you are making sound choices, especially in regard to experimental or methodological design and plans for qualitative or quantitative analysis.

Preparing for an interview

Once you have decided whether to apply for an advertised project or whether you want to obtain funding for a project of your own design, you will usually find that an interview forms part of the application process. Interviews for advertised projects are more likely to be formal than if you have already contacted someone about applying for funding with them, but, either way, they can take several different formats: face to face, over the phone as a teleconference, or perhaps over the Internet using facilities such as Skype, for example. Be prepared for more than one person to be there.

It is advisable to do some preparation for your interview. General interview preparation still applies in this situation, so make sure you have suitable clothes to wear, that you know how to get to the venue and that you get there on time (if not a little early!). Get interview practice, even if it is just general interview technique. You could perhaps arrange this through your current university's careers service or ask a more experienced colleague for some help. You will need to be able to discuss the topic of your PhD project; check whether or not you are expected to give a short presentation. Whenever you talk about the project, be enthusiastic and positive. Get a copy of an advertised project description (if there is one), be aware of the key literature and have your own ideas about how to approach the project and how to take it forward. See if you can link this into what is already being done in that department. If you are asked to give a presentation, make sure you know what format this should take – for example, PowerPoint – and if there is a time limit or maximum number of slides. If there is a limit, make sure you stick to it. You are likely to be asked specific questions about your approach to the project, so be prepared to discuss your ideas about methodology or experimental design, participant recruitment and statistical analysis and so on. Be aware of your potential supervisors' most recent publications and make sure you are able to discuss them and how they would relate to your PhD project. Examples of other typical interview questions are: why do you want to study at that university and (if it is an advertised project) why that particular project?

You will also need to be confident about discussing yourself. Be prepared to say a bit about yourself and your interests and hobbies and so on but do not get too personal. Why are you interested in studying this field or discipline? Take the opportunity to promote yourself as a good candidate for a PhD student. Why should you be chosen over any other candidates? You may be asked about your performance in your undergraduate and/or Master's modules and might be asked to explain any grades that were lower than your average. Be able to talk about your strengths and weaknesses but emphasise how you work round your weaknesses and turn them into strengths. For example, one of your weaknesses might be that you are a perfectionist. This is a weakness because it is time consuming but it also shows that you are dedicated to what you are doing and work hard, which is a strength. You need to be able to emphasise the skills you already have which will help your studies and show an awareness of areas you will need to brush up on. Similarly, you should be able to talk critically about your previous research experience whether as a student or as a research assistant. Also, be prepared to discuss your future career plans, even if you only have a general idea of what you want to do at the moment.

As well as having to answer questions during your interview, it is important that you go in armed with a few questions of your own to ask. As the interview draws to its conclusion, interviewers often give you an opportunity to ask questions. Have several different ones in mind so that you will still have something to ask even if some of the questions get answered during the course of the interview. Examples of questions to ask are: what teaching opportunities are available, what development opportunities are available, what kind of support is available within your group, for example technicians, post-docs, and other students, and how much autonomy can you expect?

So, you have made it to the end of the interview, but what happens next? In some cases you might receive a decision on the same day. If this is the case, you might be shown around the department or get a tour of the facilities from another member of staff while the interview panel discuss your interview performance and make their decision. However, be prepared to be patient as you might have to wait a little while to hear about the outcome of the interview, especially if there are several other candidates to be seen. If the interviewers do not say when you should expect to hear, be sure to ask them.

Living arrangements

Living arrangements are another important consideration when choosing where to undertake your studies. Universities often provide a small amount of postgraduate accommodation so have a look on the university website to see what is available. Consider what your priorities are in regard to your living arrangements. Would you prefer to be in university accommodation where you might pay one fee for the year with all bills and food included or would you prefer a little more flexibility?

Universities often provide some guidance about private accommodation in the area too. Again, think about what is most important to you. Are you constrained by price? This might affect which areas you can afford to consider. Do you want to be close to the university or close to local amenities? When considering private accommodation it is important to recognise the difference between student lets and professional lets. Student lets are signed up for several months in advance and are often not maintained to as high a standard as other rental properties. In addition, the student areas tend to be noisier. It is usually possible to get shorter-term young professional lets rather

😊 Inside view

After my undergraduate degree I chose to do the MRes [Master of Research] to get more experience for a career in science. I had no knowledge of the area so I decided that living in postgraduate accommodation would be the best option in terms of accessibility to the university and the city, thus giving me a chance to get to know the area before moving to private rented accommodation. The postgraduate accommodation was extremely convenient, being 5–10 minutes away from the university and the city centre, making it easy to get around. It was also a good way to meet a lot of people from around the globe, as postgraduate accommodation is predominantly international students. The bad points were not having much living or kitchen space. The set-up involved a small room with a small kitchen shared by four people, which made it crowded at times. Even though I got to know quite a few people while I was there, due to the isolated nature of the rooms it was easy to feel lonely there. It was the main reason that I moved out to private rented accommodation; a shared flat space is my preference rather than a single room with nowhere to relax after a long day. Also, postgraduate accommodation may have all bills and costs included in rent costs but I think overall it ended up more expensive than sharing a flat. Basically, you are paying for convenience.

Upon the completion of my MRes I started my PhD programme, but prior to this I looked extensively for a suitable flat. Budgeting for a top rent of £300 per month and looking for a flat within 20 minutes of the university and city centre were key priorities for me. Myself and another PhD student decided to rent together. Something important to consider is a suitable flatmate as life is going to be stressful enough during the next three years so you do not want stress at home. The flat that I moved into was nice enough at first but several problems arose during the course of the year that I stayed there. It was lovely to have space to relax in and a living room to chill out in. During the summer that we moved in it seemed to be quite a quiet area and street with not far to walk to the grocery shop. Once the undergraduate students came back for the new academic year it became clear that most of the houses around us were student lets, so lots of noise was generated on a nightly basis. Notable incidents included a 4 a.m. rave that occurred in the flat above ours which actually made the ceiling shake, and the weekly deluge of rubbish chucked into the backyard by neighbours. Despite stating that we wanted a young professional property, we ended up in a very student area and it became clear that the property itself was far from perfect. Always check the area around where you are looking and make sure it is a professional flat as these are usually held to a better standard.

> Upon moving out of that flat I went to a much quieter area, well away from the student-dense areas, and the difference could not have been greater. I have been here for two years now and count this place as my home, which is something I have not been able to say since I first went to university six years ago. Doing a PhD is going to take its toll on a lot of aspects of your life, with stress and pressure ever present, so you want to make sure that when you go home you can switch off.
>
> *Ben, 25*

than student properties, so if you do not like the accommodation or you are not sure about the area you can move on to somewhere else. Similarly, if you are new to the area a shorter-term let gives you time to get to know the area and make new friends, allowing you to look to live with someone you know rather than several strangers. When considering a professional let, make sure to check whether it is furnished or unfurnished.

Once you have made a decision on where to live, do not forget about the practical arrangements. Full-time students are exempt from council tax but please see **www.gov.uk/council-tax** for the full exemption criteria. Your local council website should provide information on this as well as many other things, such as the rubbish and recycling collection schedule and information about whether you require a residential parking permit or visitor's parking permit and so on. Whether you are renting from a letting agency or a private landlord, make sure they have an up-to-date gas safety certificate and that the electrics have been tested. Check for safety features such as smoke detectors, carbon monoxide detectors and usable fire escapes. Also, check what the procedure is for reporting repairs and how much notice you should expect if the landlord needs access to the property (usually 24 hours with written notice unless it is an emergency). Think about whether you want to get insurance cover for your personal possessions and do not forget to buy a TV licence. Last, but certainly not least, remember to register with a local GP.

Funding

Committing yourself to a PhD project is a significant financial investment. Not only are there fees to be paid and project expenses to consider, there are also living costs and the loss of what you would have been earning had you been working instead of doing a PhD. There are many ways to fund a PhD but there is a lot of competition for funding, just as there is a lot of competition for places. Advertised projects tend to have funding in place to cover fees and research costs and also to provide a stipend. Collectively this is known as a studentship. Stipends, sometimes also called maintenance awards, are the equivalent of a salary for PhD students, but do not expect them to match what the level of salary would be if you were doing the same kind of work as a paid job. For example, the Research Councils UK minimum doctoral stipend level for 2014 was £13,863, and is higher for those eligible for London allowance (see **www.rcuk.ac.uk**). The intention of the stipend is not to reimburse you for hours worked or tasks performed, but to enable you to have enough to live on without secondary employment during the term of your studentship. Note that your stipend has the benefit of being tax free. Studentships in the UK tend to come with conditions attached: for example, most research council funded studentships are only available to people who have been 'ordinary residents' in the UK for at least three years, or they may only pay university fees for EU students.

Research councils are a major source of funding for PhDs in the UK. There are seven UK research councils: Arts and Humanities Research Council (AHRC), Biotechnology and Biological Science Research Council (BBSRC), Engineering and Physical Sciences Research Council (EPSRC), Economic and Social Research Council (ESRC), Medical Research Council (MRC), Natural Environment Research Council (NERC), and the Science and Technological Facilities Council (STFC). Look out also for cross-council initiatives. Each of the research councils covers differing areas and disciplines and all have their own application processes and deadlines. Similarly, each research council has its own eligibility criteria for who can receive the awards they offer, and funds are given to the university department or supervisor rather than paid directly to the student. Funding from research councils tends to be a fixed amount that covers university fees, resources for the project and perhaps something towards training and development and a small budget for conference travel. Research council funding is usually what provides the money for advertised studentships but it is possible to apply to some research councils to fund a project of your own design. This is known as an open competition studentship. Remember that if you are successful, the award of the studentship will be made to your university rather than to you personally. Also, this type of funding may come with a contract that limits the amount of hours per week where you are allowed to engage in additional work in order to supplement your income. This is to make sure you spend your time focusing on your PhD project. More information about UK research councils and links to each research council's individual website can be found at **www.rcuk.ac.uk**.

There is a great deal of competition for research council funding; if you are not successful first time round, do not be put off. Some charities, businesses and even government departments offer studentships too, but these tend to be available only through advertised projects.

There are other ways to fund a PhD. First of all, look at whether any institutional funding is available. Some universities award studentships and many provide bursaries for students in specific circumstances, although there are fewer available at postgraduate level than at undergraduate level. Universities also sometimes offer discounts on fees for members of staff or returning students (alumni). In some cases employers may provide funding for employees to undertake postgraduate study, but a strong case would need to be made for why investing in you getting a PhD would benefit the company. Some companies provide part funding for PhD studentships in partnership with a university so that each contributes finances to the project. These studentships often involve splitting time between the university and the company.

Rather than trying to get your whole project funded, consider using portfolio funding. This is where you apply to different funding sources for different parts of your project. Even if you have a studentship you can use this strategy for extras, such as a travel grant or perhaps a piece

of equipment. One disadvantage of
seeking funding in this way is the
amount of time it will take to identify
these funding opportunities and
complete the applications, all with no
guarantee of success.

There are also some grants which
specifically help UK students who
want to study in another country: for
example, the Fulbright Commission
provides grants on a competitive
basis for UK students who wish to
study in the USA (**www.fulbright.org.uk**). For international students
wishing to study in the UK, there are a variety of grants and scholarships
available with varying eligibility criteria. For more information, start with
www.britishcouncil.org. There is also some funding available specifically
for disabled students, called Disabled Students' Allowance (DSA), to help
with any extra costs incurred. For more information on what is available,
eligibility criteria and details of how to apply, see **www.gov.uk/disabled-
students-allowances-dsas**.

Another option is to self-fund your PhD. Self-funding is more
common in some disciplines than others and some PhD programmes
will not accept self-funders at all. If you have the personal finances in
place, great. If not, how will you pay your fees and what will you live
off? Will you need to take out a loan such as a professional and career
development loan (see **www.gov.uk/career-development-loans**) or do
you have family or friends who can help? Would you prefer to study part
time while working?

 Inside view

Access to both academic and
private industry sectors allowed
me to see two different sides of
research. With the company input
there are resources available and
the chance to make important
contacts (key in areas where who
you know is important!).

Ben, 25

Supplementing your income

It may be possible to supplement your income during your studies.
Although most studentships stipulate that you may not work more than
a certain number of hours per week outside of your PhD project work
(usually somewhere between six and ten hours), it is possible to get paid
for teaching, demonstrating and invigilating work. This type of work is a

good option if you are considering a career in academia as you will gain some experience and make a little extra money on the side. If you are completing your PhD part time, it might be suitable for you to take on a part-time job. A research assistant post in an area related to your PhD would give you the income you need plus relevant experience in the field and possibly some publications too. Casual work is another option as you could fit this in when you have time available and focus on your PhD work when the project demands more attention. Another option is to take on teaching on a more formal basis. PhD teaching fellowships are available at some universities, usually on a three-year full-time basis, and offer a maintenance grant and waived fees in return for a certain number of teaching hours per week alongside the PhD. Also available are graduate tutor or graduate teaching assistant PhD studentships. These usually take the form of a full-time studentship but over a slightly longer term (five years, for example). Again, tuition fees are paid and a maintenance grant is provided, but there is a greater proportion of time assigned to teaching duties, leaving a little less for PhD project work, hence the longer term of this type of studentship.

3

When to Do a PhD

Advice about when is the best time to do a PhD is not something you tend to come across when looking for advice about PhDs. For a lot of PhD students, the 'when' is dictated by when funding becomes available, or what projects are available at the end of their undergraduate or Master's degree. For other students, though, it can be a question of when it is possible to fit their PhD studies around business commitments or family life.

Straight from education

Some students go straight from school or college to an undergraduate course, then move on to their PhD without a break. Others follow a similar trajectory but with the addition of a Master's degree in between undergraduate study and the PhD. This can have several advantages. First, you will already be in the studying mind set and so will not experience the same type of culture change as you would if coming from a work environment. Second, students following this trajectory are likely to be younger and so are getting a head start in their careers compared to some of their peers. Finally, these younger students tend to have fewer commitments, whether financial or family based, so have more freedom to search broadly for tempting opportunities. There are, of course, some possible disadvantages too. Following this trajectory means you have less experience of work and of research and so may lack some of the skills that are appealing in prospective PhD students. Also, you might not have had a chance to build up much in the way of savings and may have a student loan to think about too. This can make going straight on to PhD study financially unattractive. Finally, spending three or four years (or more, part time) on undergraduate degree-level study can leave you feeling exhausted and in need of a change of pace. If you do feel like this, it would not be a great frame of mind in which to start your PhD studies. Obviously this is all based on certain assumptions about what makes a typical undergraduate or Master's student and does not consider more mature students who have worked for years before embarking upon a degree, or young students with families. However, some of these points still apply.

If you do intend to go for a PhD straight from undergraduate or Master's level, make sure you are comfortable with what the differences will be. With a PhD, there is no programme of taught modules and no set curriculum to follow. Instead, the sole focus is independent research. Usually, the only lectures or classes you will attend will be training workshops or visiting speakers. There are also differences in entry requirements and instead of coming out with a certain class of degree, PhDs are pass or fail. On a more practical note, there are differences in the fees between undergraduate degrees, Master's degrees and PhDs, and differences in methods of funding them. For instance, you cannot get a student loan to do a PhD in the same way that you can for your undergraduate studies. The number of hours you will need to work

⊙ Inside view

Having jumped straight from undergraduate to PhD I can easily notice the difference between the workload. While my undergraduate course was fairly full on in teaching time in comparison to other subjects, it was still not the same as full-time work and certainly nothing like the time you are required to spend on a PhD project. The real learning curve for me, however, was that, for the first time in my academic life, I was totally responsible for the progression and outcomes of my project. My whole research group were very good at encouraging me, especially in the early stages of the project, but for the first six months it was a little overwhelming.

Rebecca, 23

increases at each level. As a Master's student you will need to put in more hours than as an undergraduate, and as a PhD student you will need to put in more work still. The level of independent learning you will need to carry out is graduated in the same way. As an undergraduate you are learning what is already known, but as a PhD student you are expected to discover new knowledge. As a PhD student you will have the added pressures of publication and possibly also public engagement, which will have been the exception rather than the rule at undergraduate level. You may also find that other students' motivation for following the same programme has changed too, as well as their attitude towards their degree in general. PhD students are more likely to have thought about a specific career and will be much more focused and prepared to give up their free time than most undergraduate students.

After work experience

It is not uncommon for people to return to university to become a PhD student after a period of working. Gaining some work experience, especially work experience related to your PhD topic, has several advantages. The experience you have already gained can give you an advantage in the application process, and the transferable skills you have developed in the workplace can be put to good use during your studies. Students who have worked first tend to have a slightly different approach to their PhD studies, are able to work more independently more quickly, have a little more understanding of how their research will translate into practice, are more used to putting in long hours and find it easier to create a separation between their PhD and outside interests. In addition, if you have been working in the same field as your PhD project will be in, you will already be confident that that

 Inside view

I would like to do a PhD or doctorate in child psychology. Although I did not go straight into it after my Master's, it is still something I am interested in pursuing. However, I feel that to truly understand the area I would rather have years of 'front line' experience.

Lisa, 26

particular field is truly where your interests lie. Showing a commitment to the field can also make you more attractive as a candidate for PhD study. On the other hand, however, these students may find it hard to give up a salary and go back to life on a student budget. It can also be difficult to get back into an academic frame of mind, especially at the beginning of the PhD when study skills may be a bit rusty and there is perhaps a transition to be made from team working to more time spent on individual work.

While working

As mentioned above, it is possible to complete a PhD part time while also working part time (or full time, in some cases). As the experiences

💬 Inside view

In one word, it is 'tough' — and in two words, 'bloody tough'. It is hard juggling work commitments with training and completing a PhD, but I survived. Looking back, would/could I have done it differently? Perhaps, but my advice to anyone wanting to pursue a higher research degree while working would be to have a supportive line manager and supervisory panel that can motivate you when the going gets tough!

Aditya, 39

💬 Inside view

In reality, I am still balancing it. I am approaching the end of the second of four years. It is a challenge. But frankly, the increased knowledge base, the extra insights and the innate value of the material learnt in the process and the perspectives gained have thrown a light onto my working practice that otherwise would not have existed. It's a balance I always want to effect and it provides a stimulation, a constant opportunity to reiterate and examine and reflect upon my working practices and the organisations I work alongside. Its added value more than outweighs any sense of additional burden and balance. Sure, there are the deadlines and the times when one has to juggle arrangements.

David, 55

> ### 😊 Inside view
>
> It is challenging and can be frustrating having to divide my focus between different projects; however, I think this gives me an advantage in the long term. There will never be a time during my future research career where I have the luxury of concentrating on only one project at a time. There will always be demands of student supervision, writing grant applications, submitting research papers, departmental admin and so on. So having to develop multitasking skills at an early stage of my research career is an essential part of my professional development.
>
> *Jane*, 37*

here highlight, combining a PhD with employment can have its challenges, and you need good organisational skills and supportive supervisors. However, it can also have a positive impact on your working practices.

Fitting in with family life

Whenever people talk about fitting their PhD around family life, they are often referring to having children. However, this is not the only aspect of family life that can make demands on your PhD time. For example, you may be a carer for a family member. Universities are experienced with students who have different family needs and many have on-site childcare facilities which may offer a discounted rate for students. PhDs

> ### 😊 Inside view
>
> This has its up and downs. I find it very frustrating when I have to stop PhD work to start my 'night shift', i.e., the school run, tea-time, bedtime etc., and by the time the kids are in bed I can find it difficult to get motivated to start work again. But on the flip side, as the PhD is not a nine to five job, I have flexibility in the hours that I work and I often use the evenings to keep on top of the admin side of the PhD – participant emails, data entry, updating my references. So all in all, I seem to have developed a good balance in how I use my time most effectively. I am shattered all the time, though!
>
> *Jane*, 37*

have the potential to be compatible with family life; you are in charge of your own time, so can be flexible with your working hours. However, there might be limits to this if you rely on certain facilities, such as lab equipment. Remember, it is not just time that has to fit. Consider too whether the financial aspects of being a PhD student will also be a fit for your family's needs.

4

Ways of Doing a PhD

Traditionally, doing a PhD involved doing a research project and producing a written thesis of around 100,000 words at the end of it. Now, though, there are a variety of ways to complete a PhD. However, be aware that not every route is available in every university or department.

Different types of PhD

PhD by thesis

This is the traditional style of PhD. Students have three years full time (or part-time equivalent) to complete an independent piece of research and produce a thesis of between 40,000 and 100,000 words, depending on the discipline. The thesis must then be defended at the viva voce examination.

Integrated studentships

Integrated studentships are a popular type of research council studentship and involve completing a Master's degree in the first year followed by a three-year, full-time PhD. This type of studentship is great for preparing students by including the Master's year to develop the specific research skills they will need for the PhD. This is especially good as a transition for students coming straight from undergraduate level or those returning to study. It also has the advantage that students come out with two qualifications instead of one. However, the inclusion of the Master's year can be frustrating for students who have already completed a Master's degree and feel that they already have the skills and experience necessary to start the PhD.

I had already obtained an MRes (Master of Research) with distinction and worked in academic research for a couple of years before getting my PhD studentship. Having to complete a second MRes felt in some ways like a step backwards, as I already had experience of conducting research projects and I did not want to be a year behind my peers. However, the second MRes itself was enjoyable and I learnt new skills and was able to brush up on others. This 'extra' year gave me some thinking time about how I was going to approach the PhD and it helped me get back into a student frame of mind after I had been working full time.

PhD by practice

PhD by practice tends to be limited to more creative fields and is only suitable for students who already have an established professional reputation within their field or are actively engaged in research as part of the professional practice. Rather than submitting a traditional thesis, students following this route submit a portfolio of their work, alongside a personal commentary which critically appraises their work and discusses the value of the contribution their work has made to their field.

Thesis by publication

Students following the thesis by publication route submit a selection of publications in lieu of a traditional thesis. Thesis by publication can be retrospective in the sense that you may already have a good body of work that would meet the assessment criteria of a PhD. Thesis by publication can also be completed prospectively if you are active in research and intend to produce more publishable work that could be submitted for the PhD. Those who wish to follow the prospective route usually have to be registered as a member of staff at the institution they will be submitting to. The main advantage of thesis by publication is that published articles are already peer reviewed, so examiners would be hard pressed to say that the work is not acceptable or is too flawed. This route also tends to be shorter than other options because, since the publications already exist, you will usually be registered for the PhD for a shorter length of time, thus keeping fee costs down. If following this route prospectively, or even partially prospectively (meaning that you have some publications in your portfolio already but will need to add to your body of work), be conscious of the amount of time it can take to get a piece of work published. Think about whether you will have enough time to get enough work published.

Collaborative doctoral training

Also known as CASE (Collaborative Awards in Science and Engineering) studentships or collaborative doctoral awards, these studentships promote collaboration between universities and non-academic institutions, for example businesses. Students have one academic and one non-academic supervisor and the overall aim is to provide them with first-hand experience of the professional environment in their chosen field.

Doctoral training centres

Doctoral training centres are funded by some research councils and are intended as centres of excellence for PhD study. Each centre focuses on a specific area of research. Many of these centres are run as a partnership between different institutions. Studentships are usually advertised projects, but some collaborative studentships are also encouraged.

Professional doctorates

Professional doctorates are aimed at specific professions rather than as training for a career in academia. Examples are: doctorate of business administration (DBA), doctorate of clinical psychology (DClinPsych), doctorate of education (EdD), doctorate of engineering (EngD) and doctorate of pharmacy (DPharm). Professional doctorates are usually completed part time so as to fit in with work commitments, but some can only be completed full time, such as the EngD and DClinPsych.

Professional doctorates differ from other PhD routes because there is a substantial taught element to the degree – for example, research

> ☺ **Inside view**
>
> The teaching and variety of clinical experiences on the DClinPsych are great. The main difficulties include managing lots of academic deadlines and the stress associated with challenging cases in clinical work. Demonstrating doctorate-level learning/performance to research and clinical supervisors is also very difficult to do at times. For me personally, I found the research aspects of the course to be extremely challenging. However, this is not usually the case for those who have a background predominantly in research.
>
> *Ravi, 28*

methods – and the research project is informed by professional practice. This allows professional doctorate students to research a topic that will have tangible applications in their work life.

Distance learning

At some universities it is possible to complete a PhD via distance learning. This mode of study offers increased flexibility, such as where and when you want to work, and will also spare you a daily trip to campus. On the other hand, without the day-to-day social interaction and support of the research group this option has the potential to be quite isolating. Similarly, if you know you are not good at keeping yourself motivated or are easily distracted, distance learning might not be the best option for you – although one skill it would definitely help you develop is autonomy. Check with your university about exactly what access to resources you would have.

Joint PhDs

This route involves the PhD student being registered at two universities, possibly in different countries. At completion students may be given two separate awards, one from each university, or one award endorsed by both universities. This type of PhD is great if the aim of the project is to compare two separate geographical areas. It gives access to the facilities of each university and a larger network, but it will require a large degree of flexibility on the part of the student and a willingness to travel.

Studying abroad

Studying abroad gives you all of the pros and cons of being an international PhD student (see opposite). There are many reasons to study abroad – for example, to work with a specific expert or research group, to experience a different research culture, or the different fees. The structure and duration of PhD programmes varies from country to country, so, depending on what kind of experience you are after, a PhD abroad may be more suitable for you. If this is an option you are considering, especially if you intend to return to the UK after your studies, make sure that your degree will be recognised back home. Do not forget practical considerations such as language barriers and visas.

Part time versus full time

Both full-time and part-time studies have their advantages and disadvantages. Most advertised studentships are for three-year, full-time projects. Doing your PhD project full time allows you to fully immerse yourself in the subject and focus on your project and to complete your PhD in the shortest amount of time. Completing a PhD part time allows some flexibility to fit your studies around other commitments, such as work or family, and allows you to complete the PhD over a longer period, which is advantageous to some and a disadvantage, or at least undesirable, to others. It also gives you the potential to earn money during your studies, which may be necessary as it can be a lot more difficult to get funding for part-time PhDs. Check whether being part time will affect what is provided for you, such as office space.

International students

Whether you are an international student who is coming to the UK, or a UK student who is going abroad, for either your whole PhD or a shorter period of time, studying abroad can offer a unique experience. Academically, studying abroad will open up a global network of contacts, which may result in future global job opportunities, and will enable you to experience new ways of thinking about ideas and methods and new ways of approaching problems to be solved. Studying abroad could also enhance your CV as it shows that you are mobile, willing to travel, have gained a broader perspective about your subject and are independent. More broadly speaking, time abroad can contribute a lot to personal development. The experience of living in another country requires a degree of self-reliance and also the ability to understand and navigate cultural differences. It can give you a fresh start and help you to realise which things in life are really the most important to you. Even though you are there to study, you will still need some leisure time, which could be put to use travelling around and exploring a new place. In some cases, studying abroad may be a necessity for your PhD project.

There are some practicalities to consider before making the decision to become an international student. Think about all of the administration and organisation that would need to be in place, such as visas, health insurance, bank accounts, living arrangements, and even getting a mobile phone that works. Will there be a language barrier to overcome? Many European universities run courses in English, and many people around the world do indeed speak English, but you should at least have

 Inside view

The positive side of being an international student: I was able to appreciate a new learning culture and work environment – the UK health and education system is slightly different from my country [Malaysia]. During my studies, I met and worked with many new friends from the UK and all around the world. I was able to establish my international networking with other researchers throughout various activities in my research project. Every day I could learn a new thing such as language, work, research, living, shopping and socialising. The majority of the university staff gave good support and guidance to me. The negative side of being an international student: tuition fees were expensive compared to local students (I was lucky that I received the Service Training Award from the Ministry of Health Malaysia to cover my tuition fees and other expenses), and the visa renewal for myself and my family members was also expensive.

Fiza, 42

a basic grasp of the local language. Make sure also that you have an awareness of the culture you will be entering, as well as the political and religious sensitivities of the region. Be aware of what the main differences are and what will be expected of you in order not to cause offence. Funding also needs to be taken into consideration as study abroad may be more expensive than at home and scholarships may be harder to obtain. Furthermore, programmes of study may be longer in other countries, so think carefully about how you will fund your studies. Programme structures also vary. For example, in the United States there is a much greater focus on teaching and structured learning in the first couple of years before diving into the research. As well as this, PhDs typically take longer to complete than in the UK, perhaps five years or more. Make sure your PhD will be recognised in your home country if you intend returning home when you have finished your PhD abroad. Culture shock and particularly homesickness can be a problem for international students. These tend to occur after the initial novelty of being in a new situation has worn off, but they also tend to be transient. Getting into a new routine quickly and staying in regular contact with family and friends back home can help, as can making a new group of friends, especially of other international students, for some peer support in your new location. If you are considering international study as an option, information and advice about practicalities and funding issues can be found through the Erasmus website (**www.britishcouncil.org/erasmus.htm**), the Leverhulme Trust (**www.leverhulme.ac.uk**) and the Fulbright Commission (**www.fulbright.org.uk**), among others.

5

Stages of a PhD

As noted previously, not all students do their PhDs in three years on a full-time basis, but in general most students will follow a similar pattern.

Beginning (Year 1 equivalent)

> **⊙ Inside view**
>
> Being in third year now, first year seems like quite a while ago and the years have just flown by! I guess the first year was probably more relaxed as you feel like you have all the time in the world to finish. However, the first-year literature review we had to complete was quite time consuming, and also I found myself using up a lot of time familiarising myself with new techniques and optimising methods. It's exciting, because you're embarking on the first year of your PhD and learning new skills, meeting new people, perhaps going to your first conferences.
>
> *Fiona, 24*

How much work is involved?

The first week of your PhD is a period of adjustment and is likely to involve a lot of administration and generally getting things organised. You may well be learning your way around a new city or a new university, too. The first week is the time to get organised. You will need to find out where you will be working and know where your supervisor is based. Do you have all the access you need to the building (for example, a swipe card), access to the library and other facilities, a key to your office or lab or wherever else you might be working? If this has not been set up for you before your arrival, do you know who you need to see to get it organised?

Once you have a workspace, it is time to get set up. Do you have a computer? If not, will one be provided for you or do you need to bring in a laptop? For any of these options, can you connect to the Internet or network or do you need to get in touch with the IT department? What other equipment do you need at your desk? Stationery is always necessary, so make sure you have a notebook, some pens and highlighters and the ever useful Post-it notes. If you have a lot of papers to store, ensure you have some files; if you have to store confidential data, perhaps you need to consider acquiring some lockable drawers.

In your first week (or first few weeks) there is likely to be quite a lot of administrative work to do, such as forms to fill in; and there may be some required sessions for you to attend, on orientation, health and safety and so on. This is also a good time to identify what training opportunities are available to you and to start booking on to some of those before they fill up and you find you have to wait several months for the next one. You will see a lot of new faces in the first week and will be slowly getting to know people. Remember to introduce yourself to support staff; for instance, your supervisor or research group might have a secretary or personal assistant who may be an invaluable source of help later on. Now is also the time when you meet your fellow PhD students. A social programme or icebreaker-style events may be put on for new PhD students, but social events may also be organised by existing PhD students within your group. Find out what these are and go along – you need to get to know the people you are going to be spending a lot of time around!

With all of this going on, it can be easy to forget that you are there to do some work, but in this first week you can start your literature search. The start of a PhD usually involves a lot of reading and, since you are learning to become an independent researcher, asking your supervisor to tell you where to start is not a great plan. Find out what the key papers are for your area, then at your first supervision meeting you could check whether your supervisor has anything they think you should add in; but at least by trying to find things yourself first you are showing that you are being proactive about your project.

Another important early feature of your PhD is the literature review. This will involve you finding out what work has been done before, what still needs to be done and how your work fits into this. As well as journal articles, look at previous theses on the topic. It can also be helpful to try writing a chapter list of what your thesis will look like. Do not worry, this is not set in stone; at this stage it is useful to help solidify your ideas about the direction of your work. Importantly, make sure to save all of the references to your referencing software (for example EndNote, Mendeley) as you go.

> ### 〔⋯〕 **Inside view**
>
> **My first year was quite different compared to my second year. In my first year I had to organise all the large experiments for the following years and spent much time on reading scientific papers and getting in contact with companies to order the needed equipment for my project in the following years. I did not get any results from my first year as a PhD student, which made my supervisor very critical and impatient, because for him no results meant that I had not done any work. In my second year I finally achieved results, because of the thorough preparation and organisation in my first year. My supervisor understood now that the time I had spent on the organisation of the large experiments and training was needed and was the reason for the good results in my second year. Additionally, in my first year I had to settle into my research department. I had to get to know my supervisor and he had to get to know me, and after a year we knew each other better and knew better how to work with each other.**
>
> *Sebastian, 27*

It can also be helpful to start writing about your planned methodology so that you become more familiar with other studies that have used the same method, the strengths and limitations of the method and whether it is the most appropriate methodology for your research question. Doing this now means it is not too late to change if, based on this research, you feel that a different method would be justified.

It is perfectly OK to feel a little overwhelmed at the start of your project. Remember that everyone who has done a PhD has felt this way at some point during their studies but has got through it.

The research proposal

The research proposal, or project proposal, is a formal document which outlines what you are going to do in your PhD project. Whether you have applied for an advertised project or have got funding to do a project of your own design you will still be required to submit this proposal. Being asked to produce this document in the very early stages of your studies can be a bit daunting. You may not have finished doing all your reading so might not be too sure what your final plans are. Do

⊙ Inside view

In the second week of my PhD I attended my first project meeting, which included everyone who was involved with the larger project my PhD was embedded within. I was excited about starting my PhD but feeling a little overwhelmed about all the new things to get used to and all the things I had to learn to get started on my work. For the first part of my project I had to carry out a systematic literature review. I had done literature reviews in the past but I was not entirely sure what was different about a systematic review and what I should be doing, so I was relieved when in the meeting I learnt that two of the post-doc researchers were in the middle of their own systematic review. Although I did not know anyone properly, everybody seemed pleasant enough so I felt confident about approaching them for some help and guidance. What a surprise I was in for! After the meeting I emailed the two post-docs asking if I could meet them for a coffee, whenever was convenient for them, and get some advice about how to carry out the systematic review. One ignored the email completely and the other gave me a very fast, short response saying that they had had to work it out for themselves so I should too! It was not a particularly welcoming experience to have in my first couple of weeks but it really did open my eyes to the team I would have to be involved with for the next few years.

Marie*, 26

not worry; the proposal at this stage is a guide to show that you have thought about what you are going to do, why it is appropriate for you to do this and how you are going to go about doing it. However, nothing is final.

There are many books available that say they will tell you how to write a great research proposal, and your university or department will probably provide you with a short set of guidelines as well. However, in general, research proposals contain the following information: some background to show what is already known about your topic, usually in the form of a literature review; the overall aim of your work; your hypotheses or research questions; a description of the methods you will use; the resources you will need to complete your work; any ethical considerations; and a description of the expected outcomes of your work. You could also include a timeline either in written or diagrammatic format. Remember, though, that you should factor in time for a break and also unpredictable events such as illness.

SMART Goals

Something that comes in useful for writing the objectives for your project are SMART goals. These are goals that are **s**pecific, **m**easureable, **a**chievable, **r**ealistic and **t**imed. For instance (using a non-academic example), if your goal is to learn how to bake, instead of saying your goal is to learn how to make a cake, your SMART goal could be that you are going to learn how to bake a chocolate cake which would serve eight people using only organic ingredients in time for your friend's birthday which is two months away. When I first learnt about SMART goals I was not enthusiastic, because they required me to put more time and effort into thinking about my goals than I had done previously. However, now I think they are great. They make you get everything organised up front and that saves you time in the long run!

Intellectual property

As an academic you need to be aware of what intellectual property is. Just as there are laws in place to protect people's property, there are also laws in place to protect intellectual property, which is something intangible (it does not have a physical presence) such as an idea produced through intellectual activity. Universities do what they can to protect the intellectual property of their academics because it can have great economic value and can be traded like any other commodity. Sometimes, in order for intellectual property to be protected it must be registered – patents are an example of this. Other examples include trademarks, copyrights and performance rights. Your university might hold workshops to educate staff and students about intellectual property. It might not be something you are expected to have to deal with as a PhD student, but it does not hurt to have an understanding of the issue. To know who to contact if you need help with something relating to intellectual property and some knowledge of the topic might prove useful in your future career.

Middle (Year 2 equivalent)

By this stage of your project you will be getting into the bulk of the work. You will have spent your first year immersed in the literature and undertaking training to acquire the skills you need to carry out your data collection.

You should also have had your first progress assessment, so you know which direction you should be heading in. Try not to compare yourself with anyone else. Every project is different and moves along at different paces at different stages, and every student handles the pressure and the workload in different ways. Be careful how much time you give to extra activities such as teaching.

Second-year blues

The second-year blues are a common experience during this

 Inside view

My second year was a nightmare as I started teaching and spent a ridiculous amount of time preparing for that, so I didn't actually make much progress on my thesis, although I was more productive I think than my first year, where I spent a lot of time reading random things and trying to get my ideas in order.

Sarah, 28

stage of the PhD and they can come suddenly and out of nowhere. Even students who are usually very motivated, who are making good progress with their work and who are getting positive feedback from their supervisors and assessors can encounter this slump during their second year, where motivation and productivity and confidence – whether self-confidence to do the work well enough or confidence in the PhD project itself – hit the floor. There is no easy answer to this and you just have to work your way through it. Sometimes a break can help; so too can setting yourself mini-deadlines to keep the work moving so that you can see things are still getting done. Doing a mind map of your work to date to help you reflect on the progress you have made so far and to generate some new ideas might spark some enthusiasm for the rest of your project. Other people's good-natured attempts to make you feel better, because they have confidence in you, can actually make you feel worse and under more pressure. Also, it is often these same people you are worried about disappointing. It can be a bit of a vicious circle since low motivation results in less progress, which makes you feel guilty, frustrated and stressed, and this is exhausting over a sustained period of time. Being exhausted decreases your motivation and so the circle continues. Allow yourself a set amount of time to feel how you feel, then make plans to move forward. Most students find that this feeling disappears in the third year simply because of time pressure.

Another common feeling during this time is the sense of being a fraud, because everyone else doing a PhD is obviously more intelligent than you, produces better work and gets things done a lot faster than you. It feels as though it must have been purely luck that you got accepted to do a PhD because right now you are in way over your head and at some point your supervisors are going to realise that they have made a mistake with you and ask you to leave. This can be a horrible feeling, but remember – it is just a feeling, it is not true. For some students it is part of the process of transition between being really excited to be doing a PhD in their first year, to finally feeling they are becoming an independent expert towards the end of their third year.

Assessing progress

As in your first year, at some point in your second year you will have another review of your progress. It can feel as though it is taking up time you should be using for your work, but your assessors need to make sure that you have gathered enough data (which you probably did not have available at your first-year assessment) and are on track to get your project finished on time. This assessment is useful for reflecting on your results, and seeing how far you have come in a year can be a real confidence booster.

Final stages (Year 3 equivalent)

For a lot of students in their third year, the overwhelming feeling is one of 'I cannot believe I am in my third year already; where did all the time go?' It is at this time that you start to reflect on your previous years of study and might wish you had done more earlier, but it is also the time that you start to feel like a proper independent researcher who knows things! The final stage of your project will involve a lot of hours working for that final push to the finish line, but do not worry. You will get through the sheer volume of work because you have to. Even if this makes you feel a bit panicked for a while, you will eventually kick up a gear and get on with it.

Writing up

Writing up your thesis, even if you have done some writing throughout your project, will be a major feature of your final year. Sometimes, the hardest part of writing is getting started. Having that blank white screen in front of you and knowing you have to fill it with tens of thousands of words can be very offputting.

Having a good structure to your thesis is very important. Typical thesis structure will vary between disciplines but your school or department should give you some guidance on formatting, word limit and so on. It can also be helpful to see how previous theses in your field have been set out. There are many books available on thesis writing which

Inside view

I wrote up as I went. During my PhD my supervisor made me do various exercises and write up summaries and reviews of my work, which at the time I thought were pointless, and the process made me angry as no other PhD students had to do them. As it turned out, everything she made me do gave me a head start in the writing-up process and it turned out her methods were obviously tried and tested, which made the writing a lot easier for me.

Claire, 26

are discipline specific; however, regardless of subject matter, if you sit down and write (and revise) the structure of your thesis first, you will find the rest a lot easier. When you are writing your thesis, keep in mind the people who have to read it. Making all of your important points as obvious as possible will make the thesis much easier for your examiners to read. This is important because the people reading your thesis might have lots of other things to read too and not much time to do it all in. They might also read be reading your thesis in blocks when they have time rather than in one sitting, so make use of signposts. Make sure that your thesis tells the story of your research as well as being easy to understand. If you have been writing papers throughout your research project, you will of course want to incorporate these into your thesis. However, remember that your thesis should be one continuous story, not several separate but related projects bound together.

One way to make writing up easier on yourself is to make it habitual so that you do not have to 'get in the zone' every time. Find what works for you. Some people like to do their set writing time before anything else in the day. What worked for me was to allow myself an hour to do other little tasks like emails or finding an article I needed so that my mind was free of these jobs prior to my allotted writing time. I also found it important take regular breaks and wander around a bit, because sitting in front of the computer all day can get very uncomfortable after a while. I set myself a word limit target for each day; I had to reach the target before I could stop, but would not work beyond it. This ensured I would make the progress I needed, but not at the cost of making myself too tired to work just as productively the next day.

From time to time while you are writing you may find you lose your motivation. If this happens, try rereading a key paper to see if it refocuses you and gets you going again, or edit a previous chapter. This takes less mental effort than writing something new but it is still a job that needs doing at some point, and seeing things moving along can help improve your levels of motivation.

Another common problem is writer's block. It is normal to experience writer's block from time to time; it will pass and it does not mean you are terrible at writing. One strategy to get around writer's block which I have found very useful is free writing. If you are struggling with a particular section, or simply do not know where to start, just sit and write everything that pops into your mind about the topic without worrying about structure, grammar, spelling or punctuation. A lot of what you write will not be in a usable state but the main thing is that it gets the ideas going again!

Finally, make sure you take some time off to recharge your batteries, even if it is just an evening of doing something different. As the old saying goes, a change is as good as a rest.

Extra time

Sometimes things happen that you just do not expect – serious illness, for example. It is possible to take some time out from your PhD for reasons like this and get some extra time to finish if you need it. The first thing to do is to talk to your supervisor to get the ball rolling on the official processes. There will probably be forms to fill in and you may have to submit evidence to show why you need the time off or the extra time. Most universities are very sympathetic to students' needs and will make the whole process as easy as possible for you.

On the other hand, some students who have progressed normally get towards the end of their PhD and feel as if they too need some extra time. There are many reasons for this, such as having interesting new avenues to explore in your research or not feeling your thesis is ready to be submitted, but at some point you have to let go. You cannot keep doing extra project work forever; at some point, you have to submit. Not submitting on time may have implications for your funding: for instance, your maintenance grant might stop or you may have to pay fees to continue to be registered as a student. Furthermore, some job opportunities may not be available to you until after you have submitted your thesis.

The viva voce

The viva is the thing that a lot of PhD students dread. It is often seen as a rite of passage for PhD students and is the verbal examination of your written thesis. A viva is used to make sure that the work you have submitted in your thesis is your own, and that you understand it, as well as understand how your work fits in to the wider academic research context.

The process of the viva differs a lot between countries. For example, in Europe PhD candidates must defend their thesis in a debate in front of an audience including their family and friends, while in the UK it is a little more private. There is not a set examination standard for a viva in the UK but you will usually have one internal and one external examiner. You may be able to have a hand in choosing one of your examiners. There is no set amount of time for the viva to last, but the time you have available may be constrained by the travel plans of the external examiner.

Once you have submitted your thesis, take some time to celebrate this major milestone, but as soon as you have a date for your viva – and this is likely to depend on your examiners' availability – make a timetable for your preparation so that you can fit it in around whatever else you might be doing now. In the viva you will have to defend your work. This does not simply mean knowing what went wrong during your studies but being able to evaluate your work properly for its strengths and weaknesses. Have a look at your examiners' body of work so that you are familiar with their theoretical standpoint on the key issues.

Refamiliarise yourself with your thesis and practise making summaries of different sections or chapters so that you can give a succinct overview. Make a note of any errors you come across as you go along so that you will not be surprised if your examiners mention them and so you can fix them when (and if) you need to do corrections. Make sure you can talk easily about what your original contribution to the subject was and all of the practical applications of your work. Be positive and confident about why your work matters and do not forget the reasons why you picked your research questions in the first place. Remember, it is your story to tell and, as with a journal article, you really have to sell to your audience why what you have done is important. Take a copy of your thesis with you and use Post-it notes to bookmark different sections so that you can refer to your work easily without having to flick backwards and forwards the whole time. You will look more prepared if you know where things are and you can locate the point you are looking for quickly.

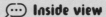

Inside view

The viva was okay. It took between one and two hours and I had one examiner from the university and one external examiner. There were more people at my first-year review!

Julie*, 30

If you are able to, have a look at the room where the viva will take place and note how it is set up so that there are no surprises on the day. Plan your travel to your viva to make sure you get there in good time, choose what you are going to wear, and decide what you are going to take with you so you are not running round looking for it immediately before you set off. Preparation is the key, so do a mock viva in order to practise answering potential questions from your examiners. There are many question lists available on the Internet; answer these out loud rather than in your head so that you practise actually speaking. It will feel a bit strange at first but it is a much better way to prepare. If the examiners pick up on a weakness of your study that they want to discuss, do not respond by blaming other people (for instance, your supervisors) or dismissing it as not important. If you feel it was beyond the scope of your project, give a good reason as to why this was the case. Take your time in responding to questions and give a considered answer rather than rushing straight in to respond. Do not take any criticism personally and do not react angrily or in any way less than professionally to your examiners. Here are some key questions to ask yourself:

- ♌ If you were given more funding and time, how would you follow up your research?
- ♌ Does any of your work link in with your examiners' work?
- ♌ If you were to start again, what would you do differently?
- ♌ What new work has come out in the area since you submitted?
- ♌ How does your work fit into this?

The outcomes of a viva are not a black-and-white pass or fail; there are a few areas of grey in between. The first outcome is *award without changes* (rare but possible). More common is *award with minor amendments or major amendments*, to be submitted to the examiner within an agreed time frame, but you will usually get a shorter time for minor amendments. Next comes *resubmit with substantial revisions*, or *resubmit with revisions for the award of a lower degree*, such as an MPhil. Finally, there is *fail with no resubmission opportunity*, but you will usually have the right to appeal this decision.

> **💬 Inside view**
>
> My viva was fine. My external examiner was hard but fair and gave me constructive criticism which has made my work better, and the changes I made since my viva will only make my work more publishable.
>
> *Claire, 26*

Finally, remember that your supervisors would not have put you forward if you were not ready. You have been doing this work for at least the last three years – more knowledge will have sunk in than you realise!

Does everything go to plan?

During your entire PhD project you will be extremely lucky if nothing has gone wrong, or at least not gone according to plan. For example, perhaps your big experiment does not produce significant results. It is not the end of the world, even though it might feel like it at the time.

> ### 😄 Inside view
>
> **My PhD research plan was changed at the end of the first/beginning of the second year. I think you need to be careful not to be too ambitious about what can be achieved in three years, and also be flexible about your original research plan and accept that it might change. You need to keep a careful check on time and progress. PhDs can be much less structured than Bachelor's and Master's degrees and so there is more opportunity to get off track timewise.**
>
> *Julie*, 30*

I have never come across anyone for whom everything was plain sailing. Sometimes things will go wrong because you have made a mistake. This is not ideal, but it is to be expected. Remember that being a PhD student is a bit like being an apprentice: you are learning as you go and are not expected to be perfect from the start. If something does happen that is your fault, admit to it and learn from it. Sometimes things will go wrong that are completely beyond your control. This could be because equipment fails or participants do not turn up when they should; it might be that relying on other academics to provide something which you had previously agreed on does not always go smoothly.

Leaving your PhD

At some point along their PhD journey, students may question whether a PhD is really the right thing for them to be doing. For the majority this uncertainty is temporary, but others face the difficult decision of whether to quit their PhD study and leave to do something different.

If you find yourself in this situation, think carefully about the pros and cons of leaving. What will you do if you leave? Think about why you originally wanted to do the PhD and what has changed in the interim. Are there any solutions that would get you to the finish? How long have you got left? Would you have to repay any bursaries and so on? Will you regret it? Could you take some time off instead? Do you need a change of supervisor/department? Could you submit early for a different qualification, such as an MPhil? Would it affect what kind of job you can get? Could you work on a different part of your project for a while? Think about the positives you can take away from it like skills and experiences. Instead of thinking about why you should leave, think about why you should continue. Are you experiencing a deep, but temporary, crisis of confidence? Will the things that are making you want to quit your PhD not also be present in whatever you do next? Do you know enough about the realities of what is outside academia to make a fair judgement? Getting the PhD leaves the door open to go back to academia. How will you explain not finishing to a future employer? How would things be different if you quit? Do not make any hasty decisions; take time to think it through. Is your decision being influenced by external factors, such as family problems, which might change in the near future?

Each of these questions will have a very personal answer for each individual. Ultimately, only you can work out what the right decision is for you.

6

Your Project and Supervisors

The world of PhD research can be a bit of a bubble; it can seem as if everybody around you either has a PhD already or is also working towards one. This can make having a PhD seem commonplace and it is easy to forget that only a small percentage of the population ever attempts a PhD, never mind completes one. Often, before people start their PhD, they have preconceived ideas about what it is going to be like. Some people need a PhD for their chosen future career, some see it as a delaying tactic before they have to worry about applying for jobs, and others see it as three years of hard work and long hours.

There are several areas to bear in mind when thinking about what a PhD will be like. First, there is your project and how much you will enjoy it. Second, there are the people you will be working with – not just your supervisors but the postdoctoral researchers and other students you will be sharing your office or lab space with. There is also the question of just how much of your time doing a PhD will take up, how it will affect your lifestyle and whether you should get involved in anything 'extracurricular' such as teaching.

One aspect of PhD research that is common to all projects is that it can be a very lonely business. That is not to say it will be lonely in terms of spending a lot of time on your own, but you will be the only person working on your exact topic. Essentially, you will spend your time becoming the solitary expert on your particular subject. There will be people around you who know about parts of what you are doing, but it is not like your undergraduate days when you could turn to a textbook when you needed help. During your PhD *you* become the expert, and there is a certain sense of aloneness involved in that.

Your project

To a large extent, your project will determine your PhD experience. Whether you are applying for an advertised project, or are trying to get a project funded, think very carefully about what you want to get out of it. For example, some students have projects that allow them to spend time collecting data all over the world, while others spend the whole three years in one room. Some students have projects that involve large teams of people, while others spend the majority of time working alone. Another thing to consider is what your project could lead to after the PhD. Is the PhD a means to an end to get the job you want, or do you want a project that could be extended into a post-doc position? Knowing what you want to achieve before you start will help you keep your focus.

One of the main differences I found between working as a researcher in academia and being a PhD student is that when I was working, if I encountered any problems I could turn to my boss, who knew either what the solution was or who to ask. In my PhD I have to sort out my own problems. My supervisors are there for guidance and advice, but for the most part I have to be my own problem solver. It can be a bit scary at first not to have someone else to fall back on, but once you get the hang of it, it can be a real confidence booster.

Motivation

Choosing a project you are interested in and passionate about will help you maintain your motivation, but losing motivation to keep going with your PhD at one point or another is normal. You will be spending at least three years on your PhD project – more if you are part time – which is a small but significant percentage of your life. To think that you will maintain a steady amount of love for your work over this length of time is totally unrealistic. There will be days, sometimes weeks, where you would rather be doing anything other than your PhD and will repeatedly ask yourself, 'Why am I doing this?' It is at these times that you need ways to motivate yourself to keep going with the work.

There are many reasons why PhD students experience dips in motivation. Being a PhD student is a lot different from the days of receiving formative and summative assessment of your work to let you know how well you are performing. Although you will get feedback from your supervisors, and your progress will be assessed more formally at your yearly progress reviews, you will need to learn how to evaluate your own progress. PhD students can also often find themselves fatigued by the process. Doing a PhD is not easy; it is hard work. It requires the production of a large volume of work, all done to a high standard; and the requirement of producing something original can create a lot of pressure for students. There is also the relentless 'constructive criticism' from supervisors, other academics when you present at conferences or workshops, and from journal article reviewers. Although this is done for your benefit, so that you can continually improve your work and your transferable skills, it can feel like an endless uphill battle. This can also lead to self-doubt. Self-doubt and dips in motivation and progress can become quite a circular set of events. For example, if you start to doubt the value of the work that you are doing, or doubt your own abilities to carry out this work and produce a worthwhile thesis, or doubt that you will pass your viva, you can lose motivation to keep working. When motivation declines, progress also slows down, leading to more self-doubt about your abilities to produce the work and a further decrease in motivation. It does not help that, as a student, you do not have very much extrinsic motivation to keep you going, as you are not getting fabulously well paid for all the hard work you are putting in and nor is this hard work a guarantee of the job and salary of your dreams in the future.

Feeling overwhelmed by the demands of your PhD project work and the demands of having lots of commitments can undermine your motivation, as can questioning your reasons for doing the PhD in the first place. One of the biggest demotivators for students is uncertainty. This can be uncertainty about the PhD project – whether this relates to either quality or direction of the work, whether their PhD will lead them to the career they desired at the outset – or just uncertainty about life in general. Support is also a big part of motivation. Not feeling supported enough is one of the main reasons that people leave their PhD programme. You are also likely to become demotivated if you are doing something that does not fit in with your own personal values. This can be a slow process but it will catch up with you over time. For example, if spending time with family is important to you but you have had to significantly reduce this in order to increase your working hours, it will gradually take its toll, leading to a reduction in motivation and a degree of unhappiness because you are missing out on something you consider more important. As well as values, consider whether what you are doing fits in with your personal ethics.

So, what can be done to avoid losing motivation? Unfortunately, the answer is: nothing. The issue is not how to stay motivated, because you will certainly have a dip in motivation at some point during your studies, but how to deal with the dip when it happens. First of all, remind yourself of the reasons why you are doing the PhD; this may be enough to get you back on track. If you think your demotivation could be a result of fatigue or exhaustion, take a break and come back to your studies refreshed. If this is not enough, consider seeking some support from your supervisors, peers, family and friends. It is not weakness to ask for help when you need it, whereas the same cannot be said of ignoring a problem and hoping it will go away. Once you are feeling better you can make sure to repay the favour.

Other strategies that may help are setting some goals and doing some planning to create deadlines for yourself. If you break these goals down further into much shorter tasks it will allow you to start ticking things off and getting an immediate sense of progress, which should help to boost your motivation and get you back to business as usual. Having visual

> **Inside view**
>
> **My family and supervisors 'ensured' that I did not stray from the path. Ultimately, though, I think the most important drivers were the subjects and their families that gave me a lot of their time to complete the research – I felt I could not let them down.**
>
> *Aditya, 39*

reminders of these deadlines will help you to stay organised and keep your focus on pushing forward your project. If your progress has slowed a little while you have been feeling demotivated, or the quality of your work has not quite been what it should be, try not to dwell on it. Feeling guilty will only be counterproductive.

Finally, make sure to celebrate your successes, no matter how small! There are certain points along the way in a PhD which seem obvious to celebrate, such as having a journal article accepted for publication and submitting your thesis, but celebrating the small things can really help you too and keep up your morale. Finished all of that data entry which has been boring you all day? Then celebrate with a cup of tea or coffee and your favourite biscuit. This may be a small thing and seem trivial, but it can make a tremendous difference to your levels of motivation. Taking some time to celebrate your successes can also give you a chance to reflect on how you achieved your goals, which will help you to achieve your next success.

Time

Now that you are an independent researcher, how much time you spend on your PhD is up to you! The chances are that if you have made it to PhD level, you have already developed some time management skills that work for you. However, you might find that you have to adapt these a little as PhD work involves a lot of unstructured research time. If this seems a bit daunting, the easiest strategy to deal with it is to create some structure for yourself. By setting some short-term and long-term goals you will plan how to use your time and create the structure you were lacking. It is also important to avoid wasting time. If there are periods when you are not working at your best, use this time to do jobs that do not require quite as much brain power, such as updating reference lists, downloading papers, filing and archiving. It is all necessary work towards your thesis, so it will save you some time in the long run. Treat your PhD as you would a job. Give it your full focus while you are doing it but make sure to keep some time for yourself.

Ultimately, it is important to remember that the PhD is *your* PhD; it is up to you how much work you put into it. Although your PhD might be

> ⊙ **Inside view**
>
> I try to be disciplined and come into the lab and university 9 to 5 or 8 to 4, as we are expected to, although sometimes I need to stay a bit later or work extra at home. However, it is also nice to be able to manage your own time. If you need to leave early for an appointment or something or would prefer to work from home — for example, if I have a report to write — then you are able to. I think it very much depends on your supervisor, however, as some like to monitor your time in the office or in the lab more than others. At the end of the day, it is your PhD and you make what you want of it. If I was in a full-time job I would be working at least 9 to 5, or if I was studying further my hours would be around 9 to 5, so those are the hours I try to work. I also want to make the most of my PhD as I can, and as experiments can take a while I find myself needing the full day to get my work done. At the same time, I did not want to be one of those PhD students that 'lives' in the lab and ends up going home at 10 p.m. exhausted; I think that it is important to have a social life too and engage in other recreational activities, otherwise you will get tired of lab work and will not perform to your best abilities. As long as you are efficient during the day — and I like being organised and plan each day — you should be able to get all your work done by mainly working normal working hours.
>
> *Fiona, 24*

embedded in a larger project, your focus has to remain on what you get out of it at the end. Some people find it easier to get a fairly strict routine in place from the start, with a fixed starting and finishing time every day and a set break time. Others have a different approach and like to arrange their work around other things they have going on through the day, such as family commitments.

One thing that I have found to be just as true of people who have worked before their PhD as of those who have come straight through the education system is that being in charge of your own time does not always lead to productivity. Especially at the beginning of the PhD, when the next three years seem to stretch out endlessly in front of you, you feel you have plenty of time. Conversely, there are students who, from day one, work 8 till 6 all week and at weekends too ... but at the end of it all they will not get a prize for putting in more time than anyone else. You either get your PhD or you do not. However, there is much more to be gained from your time as a PhD student, such as publications, mentoring experience and organising conferences, that will all be of benefit to your CV. The people I have seen do best – and by 'best' I mean maintain some kind of balance between getting things done and having a life outside of work – are the people who have a structure, who tend to work set times each day but are flexible with this when they need to be, who go home at a sensible time in the evening, and who usually do nothing work related at weekends (although they accept there may be times when they do have to work the odd weekend to keep things on track).

If you are looking for some time management strategies, there are lots of books, websites and other resources available, but remember that eventually you have to stop reading about how to manage your time and put the information into practice, or you will just be wasting more time. Do not use reading about time management techniques as a form of procrastination!

Enjoyment

It is a definite advantage for a PhD student to enjoy their PhD project. In fact, if your topic is not something you enjoy, it raises questions about the validity of your reasons for doing a PhD in the first place. PhDs are hard, and without a love of your subject and enjoyment of your project it will be extremely difficult to come through the lows that are an inevitable part of a PhD project to make it to completion.

As with levels of motivation, do not expect to feel a constant level of enjoyment during your PhD. During this time it is not uncommon to start to think of other projects, hobbies, activities – and indeed careers – which you would enjoy more than your PhD project. For the research group I was part of this seemed to revolve heavily around food, especially baking! But others have taken up a sport, started a band, or in some cases a small business. Having an interest in something outside your PhD is good and it can get you thinking about what your priorities

☺ Inside view

I really enjoy my PhD and am very interested in my research. There are times when, for example, an experiment fails or you do not get the data you had hoped for, or other moments that can be quite stressful. However, as with everything in life, there are always ups and downs. Despite all the downs, when you get an 'up' – for example, when you get to present your work at a conference or get a statistically significant p-value for your data – it is extremely rewarding and makes all the stressful times and hard work in the lab worth it. I also find lots of little motivational things popping up along the way, such as when an experiment works well or when I finally get a complete dataset. Or going to a seminar where the speaker is presenting really exciting work and gives a great talk and is really inspirational – I find that really motivating and think 'Wow, I want to be like that!'.

Fiona, 24

are for your future career. Your time as a PhD student is an excellent opportunity for you to reflect on the direction in which you are headed, before you commit yourself to a particular career. If you really do not enjoy your PhD, is a career in your chosen field really what you want to spend your life doing? Sign up to some job alert services to see what is available out there and whether those jobs fit in with your priorities for your career – for example, working hours, pay, and opportunities for advancement – and compare this with where your PhD is leading. Use this time to consider your options carefully. The transferable skills you will develop during your PhD will stand you in good stead no matter what you decide to do in the long run.

Supervisors

The relationship you have with your supervisors should be a professional, productive relationship; you do not necessarily have to become friends in order to work well together. In fact, in some cases where PhD students develop social relationships with their supervisors, it can be counterproductive to their progression and getting constructive criticism. After all, it can be hard to hear something critical from someone you consider a friend. Your supervisor might have to tell you things, for your own benefit, that you do not want to hear: for instance, if you are going down the wrong track or your work is not good enough or progress is not being made quickly enough.

What to expect from your supervisors

In the UK you will usually have one main supervisor plus one or two others, although they do not necessarily have to be from the same department. For example, if you have two supervisors, one might be an expert on your topic while the other might be an expert in your methodology, albeit from a different field. A panel of supervisors is not unusual, especially for multidisciplinary projects. The advantages here are that each supervisor is an expert on their own topic or methodology; you are not dependent on one person for advice and guidance; you have access to multiple resources; and by default you have a larger network, which may enable you to hear about more

😐 Inside view

A supervisor is there to ensure that your PhD is of the appropriate academic standard and to make sure that it progresses at the level expected of a higher degree. As a PhD is technically an academic apprenticeship, part of the supervisor's role is to provide an appropriate level of guidance so that, on completion, the student is capable of carrying on as an independent researcher. Good communication between supervisors and students is essential. Regular meetings are of utmost importance so issues/queries/progress can be discussed face to face, and enable the student to discuss and critique their work. Constructive feedback on written work is essential to help develop a student's skills. Guidance on appropriate conferences should be provided so the student can begin to develop their own research network, and if willing, supervisors should collaborate with the student by publishing the PhD research.

Jane*, 37

funding opportunities and jobs in the future. The disadvantages can include minimal interaction between academics who do not have a particularly great relationship; a diffusion of supervisory responsibility; being drawn in conflicting directions based on conflicting advice; and not knowing who you are supposed to please when you cannot please everybody.

It is difficult to say exactly what your supervisors will be like because every individual is different, but do not expect your dream supervisor. Supervisors are people, after all, and people are never perfect. You can, however, expect your supervisor to be someone who knows the literature, provides timely and constructive feedback, and, unless you are very unlucky, be approachable. Think also about what your supervisors will expect from you. In fact, you should have a discussion with your supervisors early on to establish this. Different supervisors expect different things of their students and you will be expected to become more independent as time goes on. However, you will have a much smoother start to your studies if you find out how your supervisor likes to work. You can ensure a better relationship by working with their preferred styles rather than against them. Once you are in charge you can expect people to do the same for you, but until that day comes, learn to be flexible.

Supervisors are very busy people who are often involved in several different projects, have teaching commitments and may hold other positions of responsibility within your institution. As such, the time that they have available for you is often quite limited and they cannot be expected to remember every small detail of your project. You may also find that a supervisor's level of interest in your project varies over the course of your project. When your supervisor is interested you will get lots of ideas from them about directions to take your project in, but when another project has their interest you can be left much more to your own devices. You should not take this personally. You can often learn a lot more when you are left to sort things out for yourself – but do not let a problem get out of control before you ask for help; that is what your supervisors are there for. Also, remember that while your lead supervisor is likely to be a professor, you may have an additional supervisor who is a post-doc who will be responsible for you on a more day-to-day basis, although this does not occur everywhere.

Support from supervisors

In terms of the academic side of your PhD, your supervisors are perhaps the most obvious source of support. It is the role of your supervisors to guide you in your work and make sure you are producing the best work you possibly can. They are also there to help you ensure you have the skills you need to complete the work to a good standard, to review your progress and to give you feedback. If you have a good relationship with your supervisor, you may be able to seek support from them for something that is not strictly an academic problem – for example, if you were having a crisis of confidence. You are probably not the first PhD student your supervisor has had who has experienced a problem other than those that are academic in nature during their project, and they might be able to give you some guidance about how to proceed. However, it may be the case that you have the type of relationship with your supervisor where you would not feel comfortable talking to them about problems of a more personal nature, or it may simply be that your supervisor is not available for contact when you need that kind of support. Identify who you would talk to next, just in case this happens, and make sure you are aware of what student support facilities the university provides. Although your supervisor may be your main source of professional support, the boundaries can become unclear when dealing with a personal problem. If a problem of this nature is affecting your studies then of course you should inform your supervisor, if you feel able to. There are often other members of staff within the department whose role is the pastoral support of students and you might find it easier to talk to them.

What your supervisors may expect from you

It is up to you to manage your supervisors. Make sure you have regular supervision meetings in place and send round an agenda for each meeting in advance so that everyone knows what they are expected to discuss. It can be helpful, and indeed is a requirement of some institutions, to write up the discussions from your supervision meetings and circulate these so everyone has a copy. It is likely that at the outset of your PhD your supervisors will know more about your topic than you do, but as you progress through the first year and beyond, you will probably find that you become more of an expert in your area of interest than your supervisors. This is because you spend all your time focused on a fairly narrow area while they have to deal with a broader range of research. Acknowledge this and do not be afraid to disagree with your supervisors. Similarly, if your supervisors make suggestions for your project which you think will take you in the wrong direction, say something. It is better to make sure that everyone is in agreement in the early stages than to complete a section of work only to be asked why you did it. If you are going to suggest a change of direction for your research, for example a different methodology, put together a clear, well thought out, referenced argument for your new plan to take to your supervisors, rather than just general ideas. Be sure you know what you are talking about before you present it to anyone else.

Try and solve your own problems before going to your supervisors for help. They are there to help, but you should be trying to learn to become an independent researcher. Think of other people who might be better placed to help you, like the IT department, librarians and so on, or family and friends for more personal matters. Similarly, do not use your supervisor as your only source of information. You should find out about administrative and procedural things for yourself. Your university or department and all of the documentation you were given at enrolment should give you more details about this type of information.

Do not agree to anything you are not comfortable with, but of course you should be able to give a good reason. For example, you might be uncomfortable travelling to collect data in extremely bad weather or you might not want to go to participants' houses without adequate security measures in place. Similarly, do not agree to anything that is not realistic for you – for example, deadlines for a certain piece of work, or some work that you know you do not have the skills to do. It always reflects better on you in the long run if you under-promise and over-achieve rather over-promise and under-achieve. Do not pretend you have understood something your supervisors have said to you if you do not. It can quickly and easily lead to you being confused and unsure about what you are doing for the next month until your next supervisory meeting. Say something and get them to rephrase whatever they have said or explain it further. You need to take an active role in your own learning and development and this begins with comprehension.

Try not to mess around with meeting dates and deadlines. Supervisors might have to plan their diaries six months or more in advance, so they are not as flexible as you. Similarly, it is important that you do not just disappear off the radar. If you are off sick, on holiday or planning to work from home for an extended period, let your supervisors know. Students also sometimes lie low for a while if they are having problems or are facing a crisis of confidence in their work. If you are experiencing something like this, it is much better to tell people about it sooner rather than later so that things can get sorted out.

Supervisors tend to have to go to lots of meetings. Even if they are late for yours, assuming they turned up in the first place, they will more often than not cut your meeting short to get to their next meeting on time. Try not to take this too personally if it has only happened on the odd occasion, but if this happens more often, it is a problem you need to get resolved.

> **💬 Inside view**
>
> Good qualities in supervisors are those who listen to my needs and help me learn from my mistakes. I find genuineness to be a valuable trait. Supervisors who are good at teaching and have supported me in becoming an autonomous clinician are excellent. I appreciate supervisors who are able to create a sound working alliance during clinical or research supervision.
>
> *Ravi, 28*

When your supervisors point out small mistakes in a piece of work, it can be easy to feel that they are being overly critical. However, if they are only pointing out minor mistakes it might mean there are no major mistakes, so be happy; you are making progress in your abilities!

What if you experience problems?

Unfortunately, some students will experience problems with one, or more, of their supervisors. Some problems can be fairly minor, such not responding to emails, not meeting deadlines they had agreed to and not

⌣·⁖ Inside view

I have had numerous problems with my supervisor, which started in the Master's year and have plagued me till my final year. These mostly stem from a lack of people skills and that he expects the impossible. From the very start there was little support. I remember once asking my supervisor to suggest some papers for me to read as I was struggling to understand a fairly core aspect of the project. This subject was at the centre of all of the research happening in our lab, so I didn't think that it would be too much trouble for him to suggest a few well-written reviews to help me out. His response, however, was to tell me that he wasn't going to do my work for me; it was my responsibility to trawl through the literature and he wouldn't give me any shortcuts. I was really taken aback by this. There was constant criticism, mostly non-constructive, and impossible deadlines to contend with. The hardest thing to take has been the fact that my supervisor has never listened to my opinion, even on topics that I have more knowledge of. Whether it was constantly interrupting me, talking over me, or just ignoring my suggestions, it has never felt like I've had any control of the project. During the worst times he would write me a timetable of what I was to do each day of the week, which was fairly humiliating. The micromanagement even stretched to which programs I was allowed to use in order to make figures and graphs or do statistics. There were never any helpful suggestions or recommendations, no compromises and constructive discussion; it was always 'you will do it my way'.

In order to deal with these issues I went to see my pastoral tutor to get some advice. We would meet when it was needed, but although very cathartic these sessions did not actually solve anything. The next step was that I saw the postgraduate coordinator and raised the issues that I was having. However, he didn't take my problems very seriously and shrugged off most of the problems as being due to 'differences in personality'. Finally, I got to see the Dean and again I raised the issues of how little respect I was being treated with. However, once again I felt like I wasn't being treated seriously and the only change made was the addition of the third party to referee supervisory meetings.

At all of these levels of power it seemed like they immediately sided with the supervisor. Perhaps this isn't surprising because I am, after all, just a PhD student and in a few years I will be out of the door. I still expected to be taken more seriously, though, especially because my supervisor has had two PhD students drop out and one formal complaint from a staff member in the time that I have been there. My belief is that this highlights what is at the core of all power – money. My supervisor brings in the grants; therefore he is immune from any repercussions of treating his students in this way.

It is difficult for me to advise people on how to deal with this situation, because I have tried various things without much success. If things are going badly, though, then I'd advise people to let someone know early on. The sooner you speak to someone about it (be it your pastoral tutor or assessors etc.) then the easier any changes are going to be. In some cases all that might be required is a chat with your supervisor to say what is troubling you, or in more serious cases you may be able to bring in an additional supervisor to help meetings go more smoothly. In the very worst of scenarios it may even be advisable for you to change supervisor or change project. This isn't actually as difficult or rare as you might think; I know several people who have done this and are now much happier. However, with all of these solutions, the earlier you raise the alarm the better.

Jack, 26

giving you any notice or providing any explanation. For example, if there is a deadline to submit an abstract for a conference and your supervisor promised you feedback two weeks ago but has still not responded, what should you do? Hopefully, having more than one supervisor helps (if they do not all disappear at the same time).

If you do experience problems with any of your supervisors, please do not ignore the problem and hope it will go away. It can be frightening to contemplate making a complaint about someone, but your PhD will be stressful enough without anyone making it harder for you. Where possible, speak to your lead supervisor informally at first; usually, once people are aware of the problem it can be sorted out, and, if necessary, you can raise the issue to a formal complaint later if you need to. However, your problem must be a genuine one. Simply 'not liking' someone is not good enough grounds to make a complaint, formally or informally, about anyone. If you are finding that working with someone in particular is problematic and detrimental to your studies, you must communicate your concerns to your supervisor in a professional, non-personal manner. If the problem is with your lead supervisor, or if you have spoken to them but do not feel the situation has been dealt with satisfactorily or is continuing, your school or institution will have a member of staff responsible for postgraduates that you can contact.

Having problems with someone you are working with, especially your supervisors, can be a very stressful time and can lead you to feel quite negatively about your whole experience, but try not to be disheartened for too long. These things are often sorted out relatively quickly and universities have lots of procedures in place to make sure their students are being well looked after. Obviously, everyone hopes that they will not encounter these problems, but if you do, you could look at it as a learning experience. Whatever you do when you finish your PhD you are likely to encounter people during your career that you find difficult to work with, so use this experience to help you.

7

Sources of Support and Working Conditions

Support

During your PhD studies you will receive support from many sources. Support comes in many forms, whether it be financial, academic, practical or emotional support. Your supervisors and colleagues will help to guide your project, your institute will provide you with training opportunities to develop your set of skills, and family and friends will keep you going.

Structured support

Universities have support structures in place to help students in many different ways, although graduate students tend to underuse university resources. Most institutions have dedicated student support or student advice centres in which staff are independent from the academic side of university. They can usually provide advice on a range of topics such as finance, accommodation, mental health and wellbeing, advice on maternity or paternity leave, support for learning difficulties, support for disabled students, childcare, careers advice and visas. At a more localised level, each school and institute tends to have named contacts for students, with specific contacts for postgraduates. These contacts are great when you have a problem that your supervisor cannot help with, or for times when you want to talk to someone other than your supervisor. Some schools also have student representatives for more informal, peer support.

Another way universities provide support to students is through skills development programmes. These usually involve half-day to two-day workshops on various topics, from writing skills to research design to statistics, as well as more generally applicable skills such as time management or public engagement.

Postdoctoral researchers and other staff

The university and your supervisors are not your only sources of support. Other research staff might also have completed their PhDs not too long ago, so they will be empathetic, and be able to help you with methodology and finding information. In most departments some of your colleagues will be postdoctoral researchers, while in some departments it is common to have a post-doc as one of your supervisors. While your professorial supervisors have more experience of research in general, it might have been a while since they have done any actual lab work (or fieldwork, data collection and so on). Post-doc staff in your research group have more recently been in your position and are likely to be practising the methods you are expected to use. However, post-docs are often on fixed-term contracts and are under pressure to produce publications and

> **Inside view**
>
> **It is good to know that there are other people that share your passion and fear, and that in good times or bad your colleagues will keep you company for a nice beer!**
>
> *Nadezhda, 24*

apply for more funding. In general, they are either happy to have you because they need some experience of giving supervision on their CV, or they see you as just another student impinging on their time. If you have a post-doc as a supervisor then you should be able to expect the same of them as you would you other supervisors. Post-docs can come in handy, but do not forget that it is your main supervisor you who you need to keep happy.

In some disciplines, technicians – for example, lab technicians – can be another source of help and advice. Do not be afraid to ask other staff for advice too –librarians are particularly good at sourcing information – and also the experts who run some of the skills development courses on topics such as writing technique, statistical analysis or using a particular type of software.

Peer support

If you need someone to empathise with, or you need to get something off your chest and have a bit of a moan to someone who understands what you are going through, your fellow PhD students will be an invaluable source of support.

This can involve a quick chat in the coffee room, or going for drinks on a Friday night, but in addition, in some universities peer support has become a little more formalised. Postgraduate support groups are a great way of acquiring peer support and getting to know other students at the same level as you, and they have the added advantage of being a lot less formal than talking to your supervisor. It can be especially helpful to talk to peers who have the same supervisor as you, as you can compare experiences. If there is not already a postgraduate or peer support group, could you get involved in setting one up? Having them within your department means you can get subject-specific advice as well as moral support. Peer support groups can also be a good way to vent your frustration in a sympathetic atmosphere, while getting some constructive advice on how deal with any problems you are encountering.

Another advantage of these groups is that they can be based around whatever the group wants: for example, if there is specific skill you are all interested in you could invite an expert speaker. This could be a student

💬 Inside view

Peer support is important to maintaining some sanity within a PhD! It is always good to have people who you can moan to about an experiment not working!

Alistair, 22

💬 **Inside view**

I started attending the group when I began my PhD last September, and after a few months the coordinators of the group asked if anyone else would like to take over running the group as they had coordinated the group for a year. Jo and I decided to help coordinate the group as we attended regularly and as lots of us work in different areas. We think it is a great place for everyone to get to know each other a bit better in an informal setting, and it also creates an opportunity to hold sessions about topics which are important to us and other students. The main benefit is getting to know new people and sharing PhD experiences as well as hearing about what other research is going on in the institute and listening to internal and external speakers talk about relevant topics. The challenges are deciding on topics which we think would be important for the majority of our institute's PhD students, getting others involved and encouraging them to attend and arranging a day which is suitable for everyone. The pros are meeting new people with similar research interests, knowing that you are not the only one with worries about your PhD. The cons are that it only works if enough people get involved, and you may become panicked if you think other people are further ahead or achieving more than you.

Stephanie, 24 and Josephine, 41

with a lot of experience of a particular method, an academic from the department or perhaps even an external speaker like an academic from another university or someone from industry.

Family and friends

Making friends with other PhD students is invaluable. There are times when you just need to talk to someone who 'gets it'. That said, it is important you stay in contact with your non-PhD friends, else you run the risk of spending a disproportionate amount of time talking about PhD work and issues. Family and friends will perhaps be your main source of emotional support during your PhD studies, but emotional support comes in all shapes and sizes and some people will place more importance on it than others.

It is during times of stress or other adversity that you find out who your friends are – and a PhD can be a major source of stress! PhD student friends you have made are likely to understand your problems more easily than your non-academic friends because they can empathise. At times, it might seem as though the people around you who stand outside academia do not fully understand what you are experiencing by doing a PhD, or indeed why you are putting yourself through the process at all. Be patient with them and accept the support they are trying to offer. In the case of close relationships, remember that you are putting that person through your PhD too; it is important to include them in celebrations of various milestones along the way.

Providing support for others

Just as receiving emotional support from others is beneficial to you, there will be times when you can also provide emotional support to your fellow PhD students, especially when deadlines are approaching or a study has gone wrong. It might take the form of going for a coffee with someone and letting them vent their emotions; or it might mean specifically not saying something – for example, if an assessment is coming up, do not ask if they are nervous about it. For some people, practical support means more to them than any amount of emotional support, so you could try to help in a more practical way: for example, collecting their post to save them time, or doing some printing for them. It takes minimal time and effort on your part (which is a good thing, because, after all, you are there to get on with your PhD, not help them to finish theirs), but it can mean a lot to the other person. They can return the favour later on when you are in need of a bit of support!

Working conditions

Daily routine

There is no such thing a typical routine for a PhD student. Different disciplines and different PhD projects vary so widely that no two PhD students will ever have exactly the same routine. Even for an individual PhD student, different stages of project work will place different demands on time and flexibility, so your routine is likely to change throughout the course of your PhD. Take a look at the different examples below from students in different disciplines.

> 💬 **Inside view**
>
> I have several different types of daily routine, depending on what activities I am doing. In the beginning there was a lot of reading and writing notes to get familiar with the topic, which meant going into the office 9 till 5 just to keep things ticking over and progressing. When in a stage of fieldwork, my days are very variable and can consist of either of holding focus groups with farmers, doing household interviews, driving for several hours through the bush to get to a village, or shopping for food and stationery supplies in the city to take back to the village.
>
> *Lisa, 28*

> 💬 **Inside view**
>
> The day usually begins with checking emails and planning what to do that day and for the rest of the week. As for a daily routine, it pretty much consists of sleep, wake up, walk into work, check emails/breakfast, tissue culture (1–2 hours), bench time (2–6 hours), check emails, lunch (usually bought from the shop for a chance to stretch my legs), reading journal articles, trying to cobble some results together for the next lab meeting. Overall, a PhD is a massive undertaking which should not be considered lightly as it takes a lot of your time and is extremely mentally and physically demanding.
>
> *Ben, 25*

Provision of facilities

Provision of facilities for PhD students differs between universities and between different schools and institutes within a single university. Naturally, you will have access to all of the facilities that you could expect to have access to as an undergraduate student; but, in addition, in some places PhD students get access to a shared office, their own dedicated desk and computer, printing facilities, and perhaps support from the group secretary. On the other hand, in some departments PhD students are expected to work from home the majority of the time or to 'hot desk'. Before you start your research, make sure you are clear about what exactly will be provided for you; if there is something else you require, you could always try and negotiate for it.

Fieldwork

Not all disciplines require fieldwork – in fact, some PhD students may spend the entire time on their project working in one room. For others, fieldwork is a necessity without which they could not further their research.

⊂⋯⊃ Inside view

In my mind, there are far more positives to doing fieldwork than negatives. First, fieldwork gives you a true sense of the research problem you are dealing with. There is only so much you can learn from reading and sitting at your desk all day; if you want to truly get to grips with the research you have to get out to where the action is – talk to people and hear experiences first hand, see things taking place. I find fieldwork exciting, invigorating and above all fun; I could sit and talk to farmers all day about the techniques they are using, the problems they are having and how they think we can make things better. A large proportion of my fieldwork has been in Burkina Faso, West Africa, which meant I had to learn and become proficient in French. For me, this was a big plus as learning a foreign language to an advanced level was one of my life goals and this fieldwork gave me a reason to do it. Another positive was the chance to experience a new place, new cultures and new ways of doing things; this has opened my mind and given me a new perspective on life. However, perhaps the biggest positive of all is meeting new people, whether it is market stallholders and shopkeepers that you speak to for five minutes, farmers you talk to for a few hours in a focus group or interview, or fellow researchers you work and live with for several weeks whilst you collect data. People in the countries I've worked in have shown me unbelievable generosity, often despite having very little themselves; I have been truly humbled. Every person you meet has an impact on you and teaches you something either about the world or yourself. I have made some very good friends in the countries I have worked in, friends that I am sure I will keep in contact with for many years to come. For me, the only negative aspect of fieldwork was being away from family and friends in the UK for long periods of time. As I was in remote areas, communication with home was often difficult, but the great thing about modern technology is that, although difficult, it was never impossible and even in the remotest locations I was able to speak with friends or family when I needed to hear a familiar voice.

Lisa, 28

Politics

Office politics is common in many walks of life. It is something you are certain to experience in whatever career you choose, and you have learn to deal with it.

As a PhD student, you should aim to be aware of the politics in play within your research group – but do try not to get involved. In every research group there will be a hierarchy and as a PhD student you will be very near the bottom, along with any other students. The size of the group you work in and the personalities within that group can all make a difference. If your group contains an individual who is more interested in their own advancement than that of the group, frictions are likely to occur at some stage. If you are going to approach anyone outside of your group for help or advice, discuss this plan with your supervisors first. You do not want to become dragged unwittingly into interdepartmental disagreements, or be seen as doing anything behind your supervisors' backs. On the other hand, talking to other academics can be worthwhile for constructive criticism, inspiration, and learning how to get your ideas across, defend your work and respond to different types of questioning and different personalities.

Typical pressures

Any job has its typical pressures and PhD study is no different. The type of pressure you experience will vary according to the different stages of your project, but the following are typical anxieties felt by PhD students, regardless of discipline:

🖉 *Time pressure*. Although you may not feel this so keenly in your first year, by the time you come towards the final stages of your project work you will feel it in abundance. No matter how much work you have done previously and how well organised you are, there will always be the temptation to do just a little more. One occupational hazard of research is that you often end up with more new questions than answers. You will simply not have time to answer every new question you come up with along the way.

- *Results pressure*. As a PhD student you are under constant pressure to produce results, whether for your thesis, for a publication or to present at a conference.
- *Recording pressure*. You must be able to justify every decision you have ever made in your PhD – in your thesis, to your supervisors, to your viva examiner and for yourself. Keeping records such as a research diary or lab book comes in very handy for this.
- *Social pressure*. There can also be pressure, perhaps from family and friends, to keep or get back the balance between your PhD studies and your home life.

Working from home

Not everyone has the opportunity to work from home – for example, students who need to use a lab. However, if your project and your supervisors allow you the flexibility of working from home, this option can have a number of practical advantages. You can plan how you spend your time and fit it around other things in your life; you can avoid a potentially lengthy and costly journey; and, if you need to focus on one task, such as writing a journal article, you will not be disturbed by colleagues or tempted to work on other parts of your project. On the other hand, there is the potential to become distracted by things you would have to do outside of working hours if you were physically commuting somewhere every day.

Personally, I found that working from home was a bit of a luxury. If I did not have to be at the office for a meeting then it made more sense to use the time I would have spent commuting to campus working at home. Occasionally, in the very bad winter weather, it made more sense from a safety point of view to work from home than to struggle into work when all I really needed to get on with my project was a computer. I found that I was more productive in a more relaxed environment, but I also found it very tempting to do little odd jobs around the house that on their own do not take long but that added together can take up a surprising amount of time.

Holidays

It is important to make sure you take some breaks, even if you do not go away anywhere. It will vary between universities how much holiday you are entitled to, but most places treat students like employees in this regard: you have a fixed amount of holiday you can take, and a limit on how much you can take at one time (gone are the days of having five weeks off at Christmas and three months in the summer!). People who live further away tend to save up their holiday allowance and take longer breaks at certain times of the year, which can affect the motivation of the people left behind. Attending an international conference can be an ideal time for a rest and a good way to see a new place while still keeping up with your workload. If you are going to be there in any case, take an extra couple of days to enjoy the place once the conference is over!

8

Additional Demands on Your Time

There are some things you are expected to do during your time as a PhD student that are not part of your project, and there are other things that are not compulsory but will improve your skills and improve your CV.

At the start of your PhD there will be certain compulsory health and safety and introductory sessions that are mandatory. Get these out of the way as soon as possible so you can crack on with the PhD work. You will probably also be expected to attend regular research presentations by other students and academics and also to present your own research. These sessions may not always seem relevant to your work; however, even when the topic is not directly relevant to you, it is useful to take notes on other people's presentation styles to see what works and what could be improved upon so that you can put this into practice in your own presentations. Gatherings such as these are very good opportunities to start building networks within your research community and allow you to see the 'bigger picture' of what is going on in your field.

Networking

It is impossible to emphasise just how important networking is, for both your PhD project and your career. The more people you have in your network, the more sources of advice and information are available to you, from a wide range of backgrounds and skill sets. Similarly, the more people you have in your network, the more likely you are to hear about different job opportunities and so on. Having a decent network can also help combat the loneliness some people experience during their PhD studies. Throughout the course of your project it is likely you will spend a large amount of your time with the same small number of people, so networking is a good way of broadening your horizons.

If you want to exercise those networking skills a little more, you can increase your network through a variety of means, such as becoming more involved in a particular specialism or getting involved in organising a conference, but it is mainly done through attending conferences (which is discussed in more detail further on in this chapter). If you are heading off to a conference, take note of any special groups or sessions for postgraduate students which they often have. These can be great, particularly at very specialised conferences where the senior academics often know each other already and you can feel left out of the closed circle. These student groups can be a great way of increasing your peer support as well as a subject-specific network and even for making new friends! The other students are often as nervous as you are. If you are going to the conference with people from your research group, do not spend all your time with them or you will not increase your contacts. Although it can feel quite comforting to stay within the safety net of your research group companions, if you do not leave your comfort zone you will never get to practise your networking skills. Conferences often provide some social events for more informal networking opportunities. Although these are indeed social events, remember that the people there are still potentially in your professional network, so your behaviour may influence how they remember you. For instance, do not get drunk at the conference meals or socials. I have seen this happen and everyone remembered the person the next day – and actually for quite a long time after – but not for good reasons!

If the idea of networking is as intimidating for you as it was for me, then it is more likely to put you off going to these types of events at all. Start by practising your networking skills at smaller, perhaps student-only, events. They are good places to develop your networking skills in a relatively safe environment, rather than having to do it for the first time at a major international conference full of experienced academics! Practice will help build your confidence and eventually networking will not seem as scary. The old adage that it is not what you know but who you know is to a large extent true, so networking is not a skill you can put off developing just because it makes you feel a little uncomfortable at first.

Networking is no longer only done face to face. Professional networking websites are increasing in popularity and allow you to make contact with researchers from around the globe without having to rely on bumping into them at a conference. If you are going to try some networking via professional networking sites – such as LinkedIn, ResearchGate and Academia.edu, to name but a few – remember that the Internet is a very public place: what goes out there lasts forever, so do not say anything that you might later regret. Similarly, keep track of how much time you are spending on online networking sites and make sure you could not be putting this time to better use elsewhere. Many professional networking sites allow you to upload PDFs of your published articles for other researchers to access. This can be a good way to encourage more citations of your work, because you are making it easy for people to find the article and get hold of the full text and for free – but beware of copyright issues and make sure any co-authors are happy with this too.

In addition to professional networking sites, there are other ways to maintain an online presence. For example, does your department have profile pages for staff and students? If it does, make sure your page is as up to date as possible and has a list of all your publications. Some universities also provide links to the full-text versions of all of the publications to encourage citations. If you are going to include a photograph of yourself on your profile, make sure you use a professional-looking one (not the first one you can find on Facebook).

Something else to consider is your use of social networking sites such as Facebook and Twitter for personal rather than professional purposes. Be careful of adding people from work, with whom you would not normally socialise outside of work, to your online social network. There is always the chance that they might see things through friends that you did not want them to, or the potential for them to share information about you with others that you would not wish to share. Be careful with privacy settings – or, to be completely safe, do not make any comments about your professional life on your social network accounts.

Publications

Publication is a big part of academic life, and it is also big business, but why should you publish your work, especially when there is no financial reward for doing so?

To begin with, publishing your work in order to share it with the academic community is how you make your contribution to the field and how the field advances. Further, as a student, one of the major benefits of publishing your PhD work as a series of journal articles before your viva is that reviewers for the journal are likely to pick up on the same points as your viva examiners would. By responding to and acting upon comments from the reviewers you will be able to iron out and improve your work before you submit your thesis. In addition, because journal articles are peer reviewed, if your article is published then your work has been judged by your peers to be of an acceptable standard for dissemination among the academic community. It would then be very difficult for your thesis examiners to come up with a reason to disagree with this judgement.

Another good reason to try and get some publications out of your PhD is for the sake of your CV. If you want to have a career in academia, it is important to show that you can produce good quality research which is publishable in good quality journals. How often you publish and the quality of the journals you publish in is a kind of esteem indicator of how good an academic you are. If you have spent any time in academia, or even just reading about it, you will no doubt have come across the phrase 'publish or perish'. Put quite crudely, if your aim is to stay in academia but you do not produce publications, you are very unlikely to attract any funding – or indeed get an academic job in the first place.

So, now that you know this is something you actively need to be thinking about, how do you actually get a journal article published? First of all, you need to have a piece of work worthy of publication.

Inside view

I have published two papers and am currently writing the third one. The challenges are: I found it very hard to find the correct words so that ideas were expressed well but with the correct scientific tone. Papers need a lot of time spending on them (both for the writing and the editing); I find it hard to juggle the writing and lab work. Everyone has a different opinion on what to include in the paper and how to write it, so you can get bogged down in details and end up editing and re-editing the same section over and over again. The benefits are: I find that if I publish as I go, I already have chapters of my thesis pretty much written (hopefully this will make thesis writing up less stressful!). If you have some of your work published I am told that you feel more confident in the viva and when presenting your work (it has already been peer reviewed and accepted for publication so it must be OK). Your CV looks much better if you have papers published while you are doing your PhD; it shows future employers that you can publish and have already started forming your research into publishable sections.

Helen, 31

This is not just about whether it is written up well enough (this can be worked on), but rather, does your work make a contribution to the field? If your answer to this is *no*, there is no point in trying to publish. Second, where should you try to publish your work? Identify journals in your subject area that have published related work before. Have a look at the journal's website for their specific submission guidelines. Does your work fit in with the journal's publication criteria? For example, some journals do not consider case studies or qualitative work. Do not waste your time submitting your work to a journal that will not accept it. Once you have identified an appropriate journal, read some of their recent articles to get a sense of how your article should read. Next, pay close attention to their guidelines for authors. Journals give guidelines to authors about the number of words that the article should be, the way that the article should be formatted and presented, and reference style and so on. Follow these guidelines carefully. Separate instructions are usually provided for submission of the article. You are generally expected to include a covering letter, statements about ethics, funding and any conflicts of interest, and you may be asked to identify potential reviewers. You should only submit your work to one journal at a time; if they do not accept it you can try another journal. Similarly, only submit original work that has not previously been published elsewhere.

In order to make your article appealing you need to capture your reader's interest. Do not assume someone will be interested in your work simply because it is in their field. You have to grab their attention. Make sure you have an engaging title and abstract to draw the reader in. Make clear statements about what your results are and the value of your work. Make it easy for the reader to understand the key message of your work. While you are expected to discuss the limitations of your work, make sure to also point out the strengths of what you have done; take the opportunity to really sell your work. You need to convince your reader that your work is as interesting and important as you think it is.

Once you have submitted your article for consideration by the journal, be prepared for a wait of three months or more while your article is sent out for review. Most reviewers are doing this work for free and outside of their usual working hours, so it can take a while to get responses. When the reviewers have submitted their comments and given their opinion about whether the journal should accept the article for publication, the editor will contact you to inform you of the outcome. This is the point where you need to develop a thick skin. It is very rare to get an outright acceptance of an article. Instead, if your article is to be accepted it will be done so with the condition of revising the article based on the reviewers' comments. Sometimes this revision will then go back out for review, so the whole process can, and often does, take months. If, unfortunately, your article is rejected by the journal, do not worry – you can always try another.

Some students have trouble letting go of their work and make constant revisions, so that they never quite get around to submitting it anywhere. However, it is often a fear of criticism by reviewers or a fear of outright rejection from the journal which can put students off trying to get a publication. The guaranteed way of never getting any of your work published is never to submit anything! Remember also that there are different types of publications you can submit to academic journals: case studies, short reports, letters to the editor, systematic reviews and position papers. Some disciplines also have journals that are specifically for students and these can provide a gentle introduction to the world of academic publishing. Something to consider while choosing a journal to try to publish in is the impact factor of the journal. Roughly speaking, an impact factor gives information about how often journal articles from a particular journal are cited by other researchers; it represents how important a journal is within its field. As a rule of thumb, the higher the impact factor, the more important the journal.

Something else to consider when thinking about where to submit your journal article is open access. Open access articles are available online, free of charge, and usually free of some copyright restrictions. There is still some debate about whether open access publishing is a good thing or not, but from the point of view of a PhD student, publishing in an open access journal may mean that more people will read your work because they do not have to pay to see it. The more people who read your work, the more often you are likely to be cited. More citations helps to raise the impact factor of the journal you published in, and the higher the impact factor of the journals that you publish in, the better it is for your CV. From the point of view of your university, open access publication will be important in the next Research Excellence Framework assessment (for more information visit **www.hefce.ac.uk**). Don't forget, once you get your journal article published, you need to let people know that it is out there. This is the time to head back to your social and professional networking site to get publicising your paper!

Another way to ease yourself into getting involved in publishing papers is to volunteer your services as a reviewer. Sometimes more senior academics in your department might have been asked to review a paper that they simply do not have the time to do. You could ask them to nominate you as a reviewer, but only when your own knowledge of the area is at a high enough level to be able to constructively critique someone else's work. This is a great opportunity for seeing the things that others do well, as well as the mistakes that they make in early revisions of their journal articles, so that you know what to aim for and what to avoid when it comes to drafting your own article. It also gives you some experience of the publishing process from the reviewers' point of view, so that you can write with what reviewers are looking for – and hoping not to see – in mind.

One potentially sticky issue for PhD students publishing their work is that of authorship. Obviously, since you are the one writing the paper you will be an author, but will you be first author? And who else should be included? These are things you would be best off discussing with your supervisors up front to avoid confusion later on. The way authorship works varies widely between disciplines. For instance, in some disciplines it not uncommon to have only one or two authors, while for others there might be dozens. Look into whether your research group or university department already has an authorship policy document which spells out how much researchers are expected to contribute to the paper in exchange for authorship and how it is decided who gets to be first author. One recurrent complaint of PhD students is supervisors getting their name on a paper without actually contributing anything towards it. The first aspect to deal with here is what counts as a contribution. If you have collected all of the data and written up the paper then obviously you have made a large contribution. But perhaps your supervisors applied for the funding which supports your research, trained you in the research methods you used to collect the data and gave you some comments on your early drafts of the article. Although a little less tangible, should this not also count as contribution? Again, this varies widely between disciplines and departments and is where having agreement at the beginning of the process comes into its own. Another benefit of having your supervisor's name on your papers is the credence it lends to your work. They are already an established expert in the field, whereas you do not yet have the same weight behind your name. However, if you feel strongly that you should be the lead author on a paper, you should make this known. First author publications are important for researchers in the early stages of their career, perhaps more so than for established academics.

It can also be tempting to write a paper with another student or academic outside of your immediate research group who has similar research interests or is working on a complementary project.

Collaborative publication can look great on your CV, but heed a word of warning: once you have identified someone to collaborate with, get advice on approaching them beforehand from someone who has experience of these situations, perhaps your supervisor or a friendly post-doc in your department. This is to avoid a situation where you excitedly meet with the person you wish to collaborate with, enthusiastically tell them about all the great ideas you have for work you could do together, and then see that work published by them in three months' time without any involvement from you. Be very careful not to give your ideas away.

Research groups and discussion groups

Research groups and discussion groups tend to occur on a regular basis within research teams and single departments; on a less frequent basis are joint research groups, which are often interdisciplinary. They can involve one or several short presentations of research being conducted by a researcher within the groups; or perhaps an outside speaker will be invited to give a talk on a topic that is of particular interest to the group, followed by some discussion or debate of the topic.

These groups are of particular benefit to PhD students because they provide a relatively safe environment in which to practise presenting your work, as well as responding to questions about your research and asking other people questions about theirs. Better to get these experiences for the first

 Inside view

I have found that research group meetings and separate discussion groups have boosted my confidence within my studies. Student-run sessions have allowed a supervisor-free environment, where you can discuss and review and allow for more free thinking without the worry of asking silly questions. Research group sessions have been useful in interpreting and developing my own ideas, as well as encouraging practice in skills such as presenting, which has been crucial in my progression towards being a better researcher.

Rebecca, 23

time on home ground where you feel relatively relaxed than at your first presentation at an international conference! Watching more experienced speakers give talks can also benefit your presentation skills: take note of their presentation styles and see what works best and how they engage with the audience, and then incorporate these techniques into your own presentations.

Conferences

Conferences can be a great experience for PhD students. They might involve a bit of travel, you get to see some of the newest work in your field, and you can make new contacts with the experts in your area. Conferences are also great places for you to practise your networking skills.

When deciding whether or not to attend a conference, think about whether it is relevant to your work. Just because the conference is in your field does not necessarily mean that any of the work presented will be relevant to you. The conference website will usually have a programme outline available for you to look at ahead of the registration deadline. This allows you to decide whether you want to attend the conference or not before handing over your registration fee.

When you first arrive at the conference you will normally receive a delegate pack. This usually consists of a copy of the conference programme, a booklet of abstracts for the talk and poster presentations, a list of delegates (people who are attending the conference), a map of the conference venue, a name badge and a notebook and pen, plus advertisements from the conference sponsors. Have a look at the list of delegates to see who you should be making contact with. These lists, as well as giving a delegate's name, usually state which university or company the delegate is from and an email address.

Conference presentations

There are two main ways to present your work at a conference: poster presentations and research talks.

Poster presentations are perhaps the easiest way to start becoming involved with giving presentations at conferences, because they feel a little less formal. You have time before the conference to prepare the poster and you will be faced with fewer people looking at your work at one time than you would be when giving a talk in front of a room full of people. Most universities run workshops for postgraduate students on creating and presenting conference posters, so try one of these and see if you get any good tips.

If you are responsible for having your poster printed, see if you can have it printed on canvas or fabric rather than paper. This option is usually a little more expensive, but it has the advantage that you can simply fold up the poster and pack it, making it a lot easier to transport than having a rolled-up piece of laminated paper in a poster tube. This can be especially handy if you are flying to the conference, as you may be charged extra to check in the poster tube or may have to count it as an extra piece of hand luggage.

Poster sessions can happen at various times throughout the conference programme; or sometimes the posters are just left up for the duration of the conference for people to come and look at as and when they have time available. Usually, only interested parties will come to look at your poster, but this provides opportunities for more in-depth discussion and a chance to network. If you are going to present a poster, make sure it is eye-catching and not crowded with too much information. Make yourself available during as many poster sessions as possible so that you can attract people to visit your poster and present it to them. Take some A4 colour versions of your poster for people to take away with them and make sure your contact details are included somewhere.

Research talks are sometimes seen as a little more prestigious than poster presentations. Except for the larger talks by invited speakers, research talks tend to last around 10 or 15 minutes, including time for questions, and usually involve a PowerPoint presentation or equivalent. Because talks are attended by a wider audience than the selective poster audience, you may also be talking to people who are not greatly interested in your work or who disagree with the rationale for your work or the methodology and so on. The first time you come face to face with someone who is essentially a stranger criticising your work, and not necessarily in a constructive way, can be very disheartening, especially if you do not have anyone more experienced by your side to help argue your corner. Try not to be downhearted. First of all, can you take anything constructive from what they have said? Have they identified any weaknesses in your work which you could improve upon in order to strengthen the quality of your research projects as a whole? Second, if you want to be an academic, you are going to have to learn how to deal with this kind of criticism. As in all walks of life, in academia you will come across the occasional person who is only interested in putting others down. When faced with these people, maintain your professionalism.

If you are going to be giving an oral presentation, follow any guidelines about length of time and number of slides very carefully. Make sure you have an appropriate number of slides so that you are not having to rush through the presentation. Also, think about what you are going to say alongside the slides. Simply reading whatever is on the screen is very boring for your audience. Prepare your talk well in advance so that you have time before the conference to practise, practise, practise! Whether this means in front of other PhD students, the rest of your research group, or family and friends, take every opportunity to practise in front of anyone and everyone. Time yourself, too. One of the most annoying mistakes someone can make during their conference talk is to spend forever going over the background of a topic, only to have to skip the slides with the actual data on because they have run out of time. There is no substitute for practising out loud to an audience. This way, you can get feedback and iron out the problems in advance of the real thing.

Talks given by other people are a good opportunity for you to practise asking questions, especially when the talk has a close bearing to your own research. There may be times when you do not agree with something the presenter has said. If this is the case, it is good conference etiquette to avoid being negative or confrontational and instead ask questions in a constructive manner.

No matter whether your presentation takes the form of a poster or a talk, remember to prepare well, engage with your audience and try to keep their interest. Make it easy for your audience to see what the take-home message of your work is. If you find yourself on the receiving end

---

⟨⋯⟩ Inside view

I have given both talks and posters at conferences. I prefer to give a talk but here is my list of pros and cons for both.

Poster pros: Simple to present; not too stressful (compared to a talk); you have a chance to have an in-depth conversation with interested people; you will only be speaking to interested people; there are lots of posters (safety in numbers!).

Poster cons: You have to stand by your poster for a long time. Sometimes poster sessions are poorly designed, so attracting an audience is very hard. Making an attractive poster can be very challenging unless you have a project which requires you to have lots of images/diagrams. If your work is not mainstream, you might not get a lot of visitors. You cannot stand by your poster every second of the day, so you might miss that one important person. Often you will want to talk to people about their posters in the same session as you have to stand by yours.

Talk pros: It takes much less time to present a talk than have a poster session; a talk will reach a much wider audience than your poster; a talk can have much more impact and generate more conversations about your research. I think it is easier to present work in a talk than a poster format as you have more room to explain methods, can present more results, and so on. Giving a talk makes you much more visible at the conference (which might help your career and the chance of future collaboration). If you give a good talk you will be thought of as a 'good speaker' and potentially invited to speak at more events. I don't think anyone has ever said, 'Oh, we should invite that person to give a poster at the next conference', but they have said that about talks.

Talk cons: Talks are stressful. You need a substantial body of data to present (a 'complete story'), otherwise the talk can look disjointed. You often have only 10 or 15 minutes, which is a short time to present your work fully. If you do badly you might not get invited to give other talks. They are quite hard to get, unless you are almost at the end of your PhD when you are more likely to have that 'complete story'.

Helen, 31

of difficult questions, do not get defensive. Remain open minded and rise to the challenge!

Chances are you will have experienced performance anxiety around giving a presentation at some point in the past. It is perfectly normal to be anxious but you do not want it to take over. Practice is the key. There is plenty of guidance available on strategies for reducing this anxiety. This is why it is important to take all the opportunities you can to give presentations, especially if they make you nervous, because this is how you learn to manage and reduce your anxiety. Better to do this in the 'friendly' environment of your research group than trying to figure out what works for you moments before your first conference presentation. Think positively and relax physically; avoid caffeine. It is also important to have confidence in what you are presenting: if you do not, why should you expect your audience to? Reward yourself afterwards no matter how well you think it went.

Aside from making new contacts and giving presentations, there are a few practical aspects of attending conferences to consider:

- First of all, who will pay for your conference registration, hotel accommodation, meals, travel and so on? In some universities, even when you have funding in place that will cover these expenses, you are expected to pay for it all up front and claim the money back at a later date. Do you have the resources to do this?
- Second, although there may be cheaper options in the area, staying at the conference hotel and attending the conference meals and social activities are a great way of meeting new people to add to your network of contacts, or even make some new friends!
- Third, be careful about attending too many conferences. The days spent at the conference plus travelling can take up a fair amount of time, so think about the implications this will have for staying on track with your PhD work.
- One final thing to consider is that getting involved with a conference can mean organising them, not just attending them. This can add some valuable skills to your CV. Consider volunteering to help at a locally run conference or get involved in running a student conference.

Training courses

Universities provide a variety of generalised and specialised skills training workshops for postgraduate students. Some sessions, such as those that are health and safety related, will be compulsory, but there will also be optional training courses that you can book onto.

At the start of each academic year I received a glossy brochure listing all the courses available to me. To begin with, I would sit with a highlighter pen to pick out the good ones and immediately book onto them all, online. I always booked onto a lot more of these than most people because (a) the booklet made the courses seem really interesting and (b) it meant time out of the office. It was only well into my second year that I realised what a bad strategy this was: I was attending workshops for interest rather than necessity, when I really did not have the time to spare for this indulgence. Only go to workshops that will directly benefit your project.

Teaching

Another thing that looks great on your CV is teaching experience, although this may be a conditional part of your studentship in any case at some institutions. If you are entertaining the thought of being a lecturer eventually, then it would be an advantage to start getting some teaching experience during your PhD. Not only can you make a little money and get some experience, but you also get the right contacts within the department. The type and amount of teaching experience available differs between departments, but you tend to start in seminars and tutorials rather than giving lectures. In the case of seminars, you are more closely involved with a smaller group of students and need to think on your feet very quickly. You may also be able to take on some marking, or it may be a requirement of working on a particular unit. It is unlikely you will be involved in a pastoral role, but because you are probably closer to their age and not a 'proper' lecturer, you may seem more approachable as a first point of contact for a student having problems.

This can be a very delicate situation and not within your remit, so be sympathetic and help by referring them to the most suitable person.

Teaching can be great because it gives you a taster of a possible future career and can help you be more certain about what you want to do next, but be aware of the amount of time your teaching responsibilities will take up. Do not let the extra cash tempt you into taking on more teaching hours than you can reasonably manage without getting behind on your project work. It might be nice to have a little extra money, but make sure this is not at the expense of your PhD studies! The university might expect you to do some training before you can start, but why not see if you can do some accredited training as well?

The Higher Education Academy (**www.heacademy.ac.uk**) provides a fairly detailed document about teaching as a PhD student. It covers finding teaching opportunities, planning sessions, running activities in seminars, and solutions to commonly encountered problems, plus a small amount of information on theories of learning.

Awards

Thinking about your CV again, are there any awards for which you could apply? Awards will look great on your CV, and can include receiving a bursary from a conference, getting a travel grant award, getting some kind of presentation prize or attracting funding. By attracting additional funding or receiving awards, you show that you are worth investing in and are likely to attract more of the same in the future.

Public engagement

Public engagement is not a new thing, but it is becoming increasingly prominent and is sometimes a requirement of your funding. It involves explaining your specialist work to the general public. So, where you are used to talking in technical academic language to others in the same field as you, here you will need to be able to communicate on a different level for a general audience.

Getting involved with public engagement is great way to show diversity in your communication and presentation skills and, besides, it can also be a lot of fun. You will need to understand how your work fits into the bigger picture and how and why it matters to the lives of your audience. You will also need to be able to explain in a non-technical way what the practical outcomes of your work are. Learning to present your work in such a manner is a useful exercise in itself because it will highlight any gaps in your work. By interacting with the general public you have the potential to foster someone else's interest in your subject. You will often get asked questions that get you thinking in a new way and go on to guide some of your future work. You should be able to identify public engagement opportunities through your university, but be very careful if you end up dealing with the media, and certainly do not go off and do this without getting advice from your supervisors first.

9

Life Outside of the PhD

Life outside of the PhD will, of course, vary according to many different factors and personal circumstances. As a PhD student, one of the most important things to remember is that you should have a life outside of your project!

Leisure

Make sure to keep some time for yourself and your hobbies and interests. It is your leisure time, so do precisely what you want with it – just make sure you have some. This is not to say there won't be times during your PhD when your project work has to take priority, but it is important to take a break from your work from time to time to rest and unwind, otherwise you will become less and less productive as time goes on, no matter how many hours you put in. Use those time management skills. If you cannot afford to take any time off from your project work, you are doing something wrong somewhere.

> ### ⊙ Inside view
> I find that usually I have time to do the things I want to do on evenings and weekends, but I do not know if this is because I am still in the fairly early stages of my PhD. I think I am fortunate because the nature of my project means that I can plan most of my experiments to take place during normal working hours.
>
> *Helen, 24*

Finances

Earlier, we talked about finances in relation to getting your PhD funded, but what about your personal finances? Being a PhD student is not financially rewarding. This might not be such a big adjustment for you if you are coming from a background of being a student, but if you have been in paid employment it might be a shock to the system to suddenly be living on half your previous earnings, if you are lucky enough to have a studentship, or possibly nothing at all. You may have to make some adjustments to your lifestyle to reflect these changes in income.

If you find yourself wondering how best to manage your money, your university's student advice centre may be able to give you some help; they are likely to start by recommending a budget. However, if you find yourself in exceptional circumstances, your student advice centre will also be able to help with pointing you in the direction of help such as hardship funds, bursaries and so on.

Remember that student discounts are not just for undergraduates! You can get some great discounts at various shops and restaurants, usually of 10 to 20 per cent, by showing your student card; and entertainment venues such as cinemas usually do deals for students. Voucher code websites can be excellent for this sort of thing, too. Websites like eBay, Freecycle and Gumtree can be good places to get things you need cheaply – or even, in some cases, for free. Does your area have a local market you could visit? Markets can be cheaper than supermarkets and can also make for a fun day out.

Keep track of your expenses to see exactly how much you are spending on what. Do you need to buy that textbook or is there a copy available in the library? If you are going to buy it, could you get a used copy instead of a brand new one? There are other practical things you could consider as well, such as transport. Do you really need expensive items that tend to eat up money, such as a car? Think about fuel, insurance, maintenance and parking. Could you walk or cycle to save money instead of using public transport (although if you are going to cycle, please invest in some safety gear!)? Investigate what your bank or building society could help you with, too. Do you want an account with no overdraft to stop you getting into debt or do you need that cushion of emergency funds?

As pointed out above, getting some work as a tutor, demonstrator or invigilator can be a great way to boost your income during your studies. There are other ways to use your free time to make a little extra money, such as getting paid for completing online surveys, but this type of work does not tend to pay much and can cost a lot in terms of your time. Other people have gone further and even started their own business while still being a full-time PhD student. Whatever it is you fancy doing for a little extra cash, make sure it is not at the expense of your studies, or in breach of the terms of your studentship.

Relationships

PhDs are a major source of stress, and stress can affect all kinds of relationships, whether with family, friends or partners. It can be hard for those who have not done a PhD to understand exactly what you are going through. They might not know how best to support you. It can also be a little intimidating for some people that you are doing a PhD.

Another aspect of PhDs that can put a strain on relationships is time. There will be periods throughout your studies when the vast majority of your time is devoted to your PhD, leaving you just enough for eating and sleeping and not much else. People who have not been through this process may not understand this. However, it can help those around you to feel more included by sharing your electronic calendar, if you use one, so that they can see when you are busy. If you know you have a busy period coming up, let people know in advance that you might be off the radar for a while; this way, they will be more understanding if you don't get in touch for a while. However, even when you are busy with your work it is still important to let off steam every now and then. Different things work for different people, but whatever you enjoy doing with friends and family, have things planned that you can look forward to. Similarly, it can help ease potential friction with those at home if you can commit to being home by a certain time, coming home a bit earlier on a certain night or making sure you spend at least one weekend a month entirely work free.

Looking after yourself

Finding a balance

Working excessively long hours and getting really tired will result in you not being as productive as you would be by working fewer hours per week and getting a decent break in the evenings and at weekends. Consistently working long hours can contribute to burning out, and that will not get you anywhere fast. It's a cliché, but true: it is essential for your wellbeing that you keep a balance between your PhD work and your life outside of it.

 Inside view

Maintain a good work/life balance. There is an expectation that everyone should work long days plus both days at the weekend, which I do not think is healthy for the individual. If you have to come in the odd weekend then that is fine, it is part of the job. However, it should just be an occasional occurrence; in the end your wellbeing is more important than a couple of results.

Alistair, 22

Stress

It is also important to learn to how to deal with stress. I would challenge even the most laid-back person in the world not to feel any kind of stress, anxiety or time pressure during a PhD. Every once in a while a little bit of stress is manageable, but if it is something you feel almost constantly then something needs to change before you make yourself physically ill.

You need to find out what works best for you in dealing with stress, but you could try:

- ♻ improving your time management;
- ♻ setting realistic goals;
- ♻ taking a short break;
- ♻ learning to say no to things you cannot reasonably accomplish;
- ♻ accepting what you cannot change;
- ♻ learning some relaxation techniques such as meditation.

It may be the case that you have specific stressors, such as certain people or specific situations. Once you know what your stressors are, you can take steps to avoid them when possible; and when you are unable to avoid them, learn how to change your attitude towards them.

There are steps you can take to make yourself more resistant to stress such as having a healthy diet, exercising regularly, sleeping well, and taking some time off for leisure or social activities. If you are sitting at a desk staring at a screen all day, make sure you get active at some point too. Eat well. If you are tired and busy, convenience foods can seem like the answer but they will not do you any favours in the long run. Becoming unhealthy and unfit will not make your PhD work easier. A degree is not worth your health. If you think you are struggling, get help early.

> ### 😐 Inside view
>
> **Fear gives rise to stress. Personally, my biggest fear was that I will never make a big discovery. This was making me miserable for quite some time. Then one day I realized that the end point does not matter – it is the journey that does. Science is like the Olympic Games: 'The most important thing is not to win but to take part!' Every experiment should be done to the best of your ability, with love, care, passion, thinking, creativity. If you are stressed then you are not at your best to do your experiments; therefore, there is no space for stressing! Plus, you never know, maybe one day I will make that big discovery or – why not? – several big discoveries!**
>
> *Nadezhda, 24*

What happens next?

So, you have got your PhD ... but what comes next? A lot of people start looking for jobs in the interim period between submitting the thesis and the viva, but what are your options? First of all, while you are looking for jobs you could also be using your time to turn your thesis chapters into more publications and perhaps present your work at some conferences. This will improve your CV.

If you decide to stay in academia there are a number of options available to you, including research, teaching, or a combination. A common route for PhD students is to apply for a post-doc position.

> 💬 **Inside view**
>
> I have looked at a lot at different jobs which use the skills I have developed (everything from market research to generic graduate schemes to jobs within adult social care that are not research jobs), but what I really want is to be an academic. I love teaching and I love research, so it is the ideal place to be! I am trying to get experience teaching different things and looking for research assistant posts and keeping my fingers crossed that it all works out eventually!
>
> *Sarah, 28*

These are usually advertised for work on specific research projects and can last anything from six months to a few years. You also have the option of applying for a post-doc, or early career, fellowship. This involves applying to a research council, charity or other funding body for money to work on a project of your own design. If you are more interested in teaching, you could apply for a lectureship, but it is very unusual to go straight from a PhD to a lectureship. A teaching fellowship may be a more realistic option immediately post-PhD. Do not be afraid to use the network of contacts that you have built up during your PhD studies. If you are looking for a post-doc position, why not see if anyone in your network is looking to employ a post-doc? Your former supervisors could also watch out for opportunities for you through their networks. A word of warning, though: the start of an academic career is unlikely to be plain sailing. You will not just walk straight into a permanent position that you stay in until the day you retire. Generally, recently graduated PhD students do quite a few short-term teaching and/or research jobs.

If you do not want to stay in academia, you will have to learn to sell your transferable skills as well as your subject knowledge. You can apply to whatever kind of sector you are interested in, but make sure you can say confidently how what you have learnt through your PhD will be

> 💬 **Inside view**
>
> It was tempting to stay and get a job where I did my PhD, but in the end I decided to get a research job at a different university when I finished, to get some experience in a different research team.
>
> *Julie*, 30*

useful in your potential new role. Rather than applying for a position as an employee, you may prefer to work for yourself. You could perhaps work as a consultant on various projects for the companies who hire you, or you may want to consider starting your own business.

When you are deciding which jobs to apply for, when you are redrafting your CV, and especially before an interview, think about what transferable skills you gained during your PhD. Obviously you will have gained a lot of knowledge about your field, but employers, especially those outside of academia, may be more interested in the skills you acquired along the way which could be transferable to a variety of jobs. Make sure you showcase these skills to your potential employers.

Summary

I hope that this book has helped to inform you about the ins and outs of being a PhD student. Doing a PhD is a massive undertaking which should not be underestimated or entered into lightly. A PhD will develop you as a person and open up more possibilities for your future career, whatever area it may be in, academic or otherwise. At the same time, it is one of the most rewarding things you can do. In effect, you have a long period of time to concentrate on something which is important to you and that you are passionate about; most people never get this opportunity.

Finally, good luck!

Appendix: Useful websites

Financial information

www.gov.uk/council-tax   Council Tax
www.gov.uk/disabled-students-allowances-dsas   Disabled Students'
   Allowance
www.gov.uk/career-development-loans   Career Development Loans
www.hefce.ac.uk   Higher Education Funding Council for England

Professional networking sites

www.academia.edu   Academia
https://uk.linkedin.com   LinkedIn
www.researchgate.net   ResearchGate

Referencing software

www.endnote.com   EndNote
www.mendeley.com   Mendeley

Research councils

www.rcuk.ac.uk   Research Councils UK
www.ahrc.ac.uk   Arts and Humanities Research Council
www.bbsrc.ac.uk   Biotechnology and Biological Sciences Research
   Council
www.esrc.ac.uk   Economic and Social Research Council
www.epsrc.ac.uk   Engineering and Physical Sciences Research Council
www.mrc.ac.uk   Medical Research Council
www.nerc.ac.uk   Natural Environment Research Council
www.stfc.ac.uk   Science and Technology Facilities Council

Studentship databases (also see research council websites)

www.findaphd.com   Searchable database
www.jobs.ac.uk   Searchable database

Studying abroad

www.fulbright.org.uk   Fulbright Commission
www.britishcouncil.org/erasmus.htm   British Council
www.leverhulme.ac.uk   The Leverhulme Trust

Teaching as a PhD student

www.heacademy.ac.uk   Higher Education Academy

University information

www.ref.ac.uk   Research Excellence Framework
www.russellgroup.ac.uk   The Russell Group

Index

Notes

Notes

Notes

Notes

Notes